THE
CUSTOMER
EXPERIENCE

CHRISTOFF J. WEIHMAN

ISBN-13: 978-0692112908
ISBN-10: 0692112901

Praise for *The Customer Experience*

"I may have learned the hard way that you really must take care of your customers. It's a whole lot easier to keep the ones you have than to get new ones. But how do you do that? How do you give them an experience that motivates them to be truly loyal to you and want to keep coming back? Christoff has written THE Book on the Customer Experience. It's insightful, educational & enjoyable. If you're in business, want to grow your business, and want to make more money, this is a book you can't afford NOT to read."

Forbes Riley, Award winning TV Host, Motivational Keynote Speaker,
Author, Health & Fitness Expert

"Christoff's essence is vividly clear from the first chapter. His writing is honest, from the heart. This book is relatable and relevant for our times. Most Enjoyable and Essential!"

Stephanie Leese Emrich
Service Speaks Solutions, President/Chief Service Officer
National Customer Service Association
~ NCSA Chicagoland, Founding President

"Christoff brings to life the vital concepts of service through his stories as they relate to touchpoints, our emotions and empathy. I found myself engaged in the reading and agreeing wholeheartedly in the message he conveys. Everyone, regardless of your profession or industry, should read this book!"

Wes Tindal,
COO National Customer Service Association

"Christoff's book, *The Customer Experience,* is a great read that gets you stop, think and reflect on how you can provide a better experience to elevate your game. When you play a better game, you get better results. I enjoyed the interesting stories, examples and insights included in this book and definitely recommend checking it out. Regardless of how long you've been in business, you will gain something from reading it that can benefit you, and those you serve will appreciate you implementing the ideas. After all, we are the customer experience."

Kenny Harper, Speaker, Marketing Strategist,
Author, Rock My Image

"Being a CEO, Entrepreneur and International Speaker, I am always asked by other business owners how to get an edge on their competition. I teach business owners how to get unlimited leads for their business. But if you really want to serve your customers well and blow them away, you must up your customer service game. I highly recommend anyone who is serious about creating a game changer in their business to read *The Customer Experience.* The content is straight-forward, inspiring and practical."

Daven Michaels,
New York Times Best Selling Author & CEO

"This book is a great read! The concepts Christoff offers about energy and customer service are spot on. I believe this book is the key to helping companies create a culture for their employees that takes the customer experience to another level that will show up on the bottom line. A rising tide floats all boats!"

James Dentley, International Speaker, Business Strategist
& Author of The Five Frequencies of High Performance

"As a provider of outsourced customer support services, I'm always on the lookout for great training resources. What I love about this book is the step-by-step process Christoff has mapped out for elevating the customer experience by teaching us to emotionally understand and connect with the customer. While this might look like a book, it should be considered a tool to raise the standards for your customer service experience. Christoff has masterfully decoded the components for what creates an exceptional customer experience, thus showcasing his mastery in this subject."

Beejel Parmar, Business Development
& Progress Coach, Keynote Speaker

"Christoff has a contagious, positive energy that is evident in his work. He provides his audience with top notch content, enthusiasm and practical strategies. His book, *The Customer Experience*, is a must read for anyone who wants to take their customer service to the next level."

David Brownlee, author Rockstar Service, Rockstar Profits,
and Founder of Pure Customer Service

Dedicated to my Amazing Wife, Michelle. Thank you for your support, your encouragement, your love and for standing by my side as we create an abundant life together. You inspire me daily as you serve your team, your patients and their families with passion and positivity. You truly embody the spirit of what *The Customer Experience* is. I am grateful for you. My life has changed since the day we met. And it keeps getting better. I am grateful and blessed to share this journey called life with you. I Love you, Now and Always.

Contents

Acknowledgements

I am very excited and grateful to be releasing my 2nd book. It has been an inspiring journey for me as I have contemplated, researched and opened myself up to this topic of the Customer Experience. Unlike my first book, in which I interviewed a wide array of experts and industry professionals, with *The Customer Experience*, I limited my interviews to just a few people. That is not to say that many, many others did not inform my thoughts, ideas and process in writing this book. In fact, many others have. Too many to even begin to name. However, there are some individuals that I do wish to give credit to and express my gratitude to for their input to this great book.

First and foremost, I am grateful to my wife, **Michelle**. As you will see as you read, many of the stories come from Michelle's experience of leading the ICU team at a major hospital in Las Vegas. Her input has been invaluable and her experiences provide stories to help bring to life the principles I am intending to convey in this book.

I am grateful to my mentor **Peter Anthony Wynn**, CEO of YouWillChangetheWorld.com. He truly understands that how we make our customers feel is paramount to the success of our business. His wisdom and insights make me better at what I do well. He is a master at guiding people to clearly articulate their message. I am excited to invite you to check out my online courses at YouWillChangetheWorld.com

I am grateful to **Bill Crutcher**, President of the National Customer Service Association (NCSA) and **Wes Tindal**, COO of NCSA for their encouragement, support and for inviting me to speak 2 years in a row at the NCSA National Conference.

A special thanks goes to my mentor, **Shep Hyken**, both for being an awesome example of a Customer Service Expert who consistently shares his genius to inspire others to excellence AND for graciously writing the foreword for my book. Thanks for your support, Shep.

I am grateful to **Adam Toporek**, Customer Service Expert and author of *Be Your Customer's Hero*, for sharing his insights and wisdom with me. He both allowed me to interview him and then he interviewed me twice for his national podcast and YouTube show, Customers that Stick and Breaking the Customer Code.

Lynne Belcher is the former CNO at the hospital here in Las Vegas where my wife, Michelle currently works. Lynne kindly sat down with me and shared her insights of the Customer Experience in the healthcare arena. I have quoted her a few times here and I am grateful for her input.

Matthew and Terces Engelhart, although I've never met them, (yet) they profoundly impacted this book. When I was nearly finished writing *The Customer Experience*, I happened upon and began reading their book, *Sacred Commerce*.

One night as I was reading *Sacred Commerce*, the light came on. First, I exclaimed to my wife, "This is such a great book and when people read *The Customer Experience*, I want them to feel the way that I am feeling right now. To be inspired and to really understand the deeper aspect to serving their customers." It was at that moment that a thought came to me that this book is really about consciously creating and elevating the emotional journey of our customers. Matthew and Terces, thank you for being an inspiration to me.

Finally, I wish to express my gratitude to **Ann McIndoo**, the Author's Coach. Her book, 7 Easy Steps to Write Your Book is easy to follow, and brilliant. I used her system of Power Anchors, Power Script and Power Move each time I sat down to write. If you are considering to write a book, I highly recommend that you contact Ann and invite her to be your author coach.

I am also grateful to:

All the people who have interviewed me on their radio shows and podcasts for my first book; providing exposure for *Getting to WOW!*;

Everyone who has pre-ordered copies of *The Customer Experience*, for their support and for their patience;

Each and every one of my clients, who have hired me and invited me to share, teach, train and inspire their team, company or organization;

All of my Soupfly blog readers from all over the world;

All of the people who have purchased a copy of *Getting to WOW!* or

The Customer Experience, or who will purchase a copy/copies in the future.

Special Thanks to **Sean Butler** for the cover photo.

Foreword by Shep Hyken

Years ago, when my children were younger – my daughters were four and six, and my son was nine – I would take them out for breakfast at least once a week. I would ask them, "Hey kids, where do you want to go for breakfast?" And they would always say, "McDonald's!" Okay, McDonald's, it's a great place to take your kids for breakfast.

I vividly remember one of the days we went to McDonald's. We walked in and were greeted by the woman at the counter. She had a big smile and her arms were wide open. She radiated positive energy and said, "Welcome! Look who's here. Come on up here kids. I know exactly what you're going to have for breakfast."

She proceeded to tell my kids what they wanted to order. And she was right! My kids were blown away by this. Amazing! My daughter quickly figured it out and said, "Hey Dad, I think that's the lady that waited on us last week. She remembered us."

We sat at our table, enjoying our breakfast, and as we walked out my older daughter said, "Dad, the people at McDonald's are fantastic. They're really great!"

As she said this, I thought to myself, my daughter almost got it right. But it wasn't the *people* at McDonald's. It was the *person*. It was that particular woman who we interacted with who caused my daughter to say, "The *people* are fantastic."

You see, we all have what I like to call the *Awesome Responsibility*, which means that at any given time in an organization, any one of us represents all of us – every single employee or team member. One of us serves as the face of *the entire brand throughout the world.*

We all have this Awesome Responsibility, which is one of the main, underlying themes of *The Customer Experience.* Each one of us, regardless of position or title, has the opportunity to either positively or negatively affect the experience of our customers. It begins with each of us understanding and accepting the powerful potential we have to impact our customers.

I first met Christoff in 2016 when he invited me to speak in Las Vegas at his first Customer Service Seminar, EXCELLERATE SERVICE. When he sent a team member to pick me up at my hotel, he made every effort to recreate the experience that I had in my now-famous taxi cab story, complete with newspapers, cold beverages, and candy.

By the time I arrived at his EXCELLERATE SERVICE event, I felt welcomed, appreciated, and cared for. This is the essence of customer service. In this book, Christoff shares his philosophy that "the desired end result of any service interaction is a positive feeling." His passion to serve and his desire to inspire others shines through his writing, just as it does when you meet him in person. His energy and positive spirit are infectious.

In *The Customer Experience*, Christoff delves deep into guiding the reader to understand that we must go beyond mere customer service toward a focus on the customer experience. He encourages us, that we must "consciously create" an emotional journey for those we serve. From attracting and assembling the right team, to empowering them and enlisting their commitment to the mission and values of the organization, Christoff provides a simple roadmap for us as service professionals. He explains the power of energy and emotion, and the role they play in designing a positive experience for our clientele on a consistent basis.

The Customer Experience is an inspiring and uplifting work that should be required reading for anyone who wants to elevate their customers' journey and who embraces the Awesome Responsibility, knowing that each one of us is "The Customer Experience."

Shep Hyken, customer service and experience expert and New York Times bestselling author of The Amazement Revolution

Introduction

I have always been in Service. I have worked in restaurants on and off since I was 15 years old. When I was 19 years old, I went overseas to serve as a volunteer missionary with a non-denominational Christian organization, spending 13 years in the Pacific and Asia. I had so many wonderful, eye-opening, life-changing experiences during those years. When I heard the call to go serve overseas, I truly thought I would spend the rest of my life there, serving in that way. I learned to speak, read and write two Philippine languages, Tagalog and Ilokano. It was an awesome privilege to live in the Philippines and serve the people of that country in various capacities. I assisted in feeding and medical programs for the urban poor, I taught literacy to non-literate tribal adults who lived in the remote mountain villages of the north, and I did a multitude of other tasks that displayed God's love in action for my Filipino brethren.

So, what does all that have to do with writing this book, *The Customer Experience*? Everything. I know I was called to serve, and in whatever capacity, whether on the mission field, or in later years, working at a hotel or restaurant, I have always strived to provide the best service possible, according to the training that I had received, and the knowledge I had at the time. I love to serve. I am blessed knowing that I have blessed another.

I believe that our highest calling is to use our gifts in service to others.

After years of serving in the hospitality industry, I felt another calling, I was inspired to write, to speak and to inspire and empower others to aspire to that same level of Service Excellence. Three years ago, my first book, *Getting to WOW! Everybody WINS with 5 Star Service*, was released. That launched my company ASPIRE Enterprises and the opportunity to bring 5 Star Service & Hospitality Training to businesses around the country. That book opened many doors of opportunity for me for which I am grateful.

A couple years ago, I was inspired with the idea of this book when I was writing my blog, Soupfly.wordpress.com and it happened to be National Nurses Week. My wife, Michelle is a Registered Nurse with 20 plus years of experience. I decided I wanted to write a blog post honoring nurses as the unsung heroes that they are. At the hospital where she currently works, Michelle has a plastic bracelet that she wears which has a very simple message on it:

I AM THE PATIENT EXPERIENCE

When I was considering to write the blog post about Nurses, I began to ponder that simple statement: I AM THE PATIENT EXPERIENCE. What does that mean?

What came to me was a simple, yet profound understanding that when a person has a 'successful' hospital stay, it is not due to the wonderful comfort of the hospital bed, nor is it the ambience of the room, nor the medicine administered, nor the food-that causes a patient to remark favorably about their stay. Rather, it is largely due to kindness, the care, the positive upbeat attitude and the overall Service of the nurse or the nursing team that was by the patient's side during this most difficult time.

To me, that sums it up. Consider that a patient in a hospital is, most of the time, an unwilling customer, as in they didn't choose to be there, unlike a restaurant guest, who, usually is at that establishment by choice.

For a patient, whatever their experience during their hospital stay, by and large is going to be equated with how well they felt the nurse(s) took care of them.

I AM THE PATIENT EXPERIENCE. When that patient says that hospital did a great job of taking care of them-they're usually referring to the nurses. When a patient says "they ignored me and let me be in pain", that patient is referring to the nurse(s). The nurse is the representative of the hospital in the mind of the customer, the patient. If the hospital gets a positive review-usually it's thanks to the Nurse(s). I'm not trying to minimize or diminish the part that the doctors play, but the reality is that the nurses are there 24/7 available to the customer-the patient. They know, realize and embrace that they are "the Patient Experience".

I've learned from Michelle that there are certain protocol, certain steps and procedures that are to be followed by the nursing staff, and yet it is possible for a nurse to follow such protocol to the "T" and still not really provide great Service to the customer, the patient. Why? Because technical skills and ability without the heart of a Servant leaves something lacking.

I began to consider other industries to see if this is true also. When a person goes to purchase a new car, it is not the ambience of the dealership that they remember, or the free coffee or snacks provided to them, oftentimes it's not even the price that is foremost in the memory of the customer. Instead, it's how the sales person made them feel. That sales person, in the mind of the customer, is '**The Customer Experience**'.

In real estate, the same holds true. It's the way you make the customer feel that will be remembered. My thesis is that this philosophy holds true for every industry wherein you are interacting with customers. Yes, the product is important, but most often it is not as important as the Service you deliver and the overall Experience of the Customer.

Consider the words of Maya Angelou, "I've learned that people will forget what you say, they will forget what you do, but they will remember how you made them feel."

My goal is to spread this message and my hope is that every Service Professional, regardless of industry, would come to understand, and embrace this philosophy and apply it on a daily basis that- **WE ARE THE CUSTOMER EXPERIENCE.**

Matthew and Terces Engelhart, in their great book, *Sacred Commerce*, talk about embracing a spiritual mindset in regards to business. Being mindful of a higher calling. They stress that every business is "an opportunity to make a lasting impact on the lives of both clients and employees".

What feeling do your patients, customers, or guests take with them when they leave your establishment?

Do they feel like they're just a number, just another body, just another customer?

Or do they feel well cared for, appreciated, valued and that you genuinely were interested in their well-being, their experience?

I believe that our highest calling is to use our gifts in service to others. The world is waiting for each of us to heed the call. When we do, we will then embrace that indeed, each of us is the Customer Experience.

A True Customer Service Hero Story

O n a recent trip to Atlanta, I experienced varying degrees of customer service displayed by the staff at Frontier Airlines. I know that I am not alone in this, as recently, the airline industry has been in the forefront of the news in regards to the good, the bad and the ugly way passengers are treated. Almost all the major airlines-United, Southwest, Jet Blue, Delta, and more, have been in the news for poor performance when dealing with the flying public. My experience actually took place before I even got on the plane. In fact, due to the events that unfolded, I almost *didn't make it* onto the plane.

Before I share my story, let me say, No, I was not dragged off the plane by rude flight attendants or over-zealous security officers. No, my multi-thousand dollars guitars were not destroyed by staff. No, I was not berated or called some insulting degrading name. Mine is just a simple story that tells of my experience which displays examples of both mediocre service and Excellent Customer service provided to me by different members of the same staff.

How Do You Feel When You Travel?

These days, there is a myriad of emotions that the flying public feel when they travel by air. It is different for each one of us and many of us find ourselves on an "emotional roller coaster". You know what I'm talking about. What starts out as excitement for your trip often quickly turns into apprehension, nervousness, anxiety, frustration, impatience or any number of other not so-pleasant-emotions. We all have been there.

Touch Points

There are many points along one's journey-called Touch Points where there is an opportunity for a service professional to interact with and affect (either positively or negatively) the customer's overall experience. When I shared this story at the NCSA Conference- I began by asking the audience, "How do you feel when you fly?" They named all the emotions listed above and more. Interestingly, not a single one of them said, "I feel calm. I feel relaxed. I feel peaceful, or overjoyed."

The reality is that there are thousands of flights traveling across the United States every single day, carrying hundreds of thousands of passengers, many whom are anxious, nervous, irritated and frustrated.

Airline staff are Service Professionals. Their primary duty should be, regardless of their position or job title, to provide great customer service to their passengers as they ensure their safe journey to their destination. However, this does not always seem to be their primary concern.

My Story

I was booked on a Frontier Airlines flight departing at 12:40 am, from Las Vegas to Atlanta last April. I was super excited as I was scheduled to speak at the National Customer Service Association, (NCSA) Conference. This was my second year to be at this prestigious event as a speaker. And I was scheduled to speak not once, not twice, but a total of three times! Including closing the awards banquet! I was stoked! I had been looking forward to this for months!

Packing

When I travel, I tend to pack more than I end up using. More clothes, more shoes, more hats, more books. More everything. This is why road trips often work better for me, as there is no limit-or relatively no limit to what I can bring/pack, as long as I can fit it in the car. Also, it always takes me way too long to get all my stuff together, especially if I'm traveling alone and my wife is working. On this particular day, my wife was working. As she was leaving to work at 5:45 am, she admonished me to make sure I do nothing else this morning until I get all packed. I agreed and kissed her good bye.

I don't know what happened but the hours quickly flew by. My suitcases and garment bag were lying on the bed half-packed. I just stood there staring at them. I've got to finish, I told myself. Bottom line- I was rushed. I did not leave myself ample time to get to the airport and through security. I take full responsibility for this.

I order my Lyft and wait. I get in with my 4 bags; suitcase, matching carry-on, garment bag and satchel, and take the 20 minute ride to McCarran International airport. I text my wife. She mentions that I was leaving a bit late. I text her 'It's fine'.

At the Airport

Arriving at the airport, I was expecting curbside check-in at Frontier Airlines. Nope. There was none. I also had not yet printed out my boarding pass. I go to the kiosk but can't figure out how to print the boarding pass. I ask a staff member and they graciously assist me. That was nice. Thanks. I'm still a little irritated about the lack of curb side check in. It's how I always travel. It's easy, convenient and I don't have to lug all my bags up to the check in counter.

I walk up to the counter, place my suitcase and carry-on on the weigh scale. I put my garment bag and shoulder bag on the ground. There are at least 4, maybe 5, counter attendants, unoccupied, talking among themselves. I mention to them that I was hoping for curbside check-in. One young man replies, laughing, "Well sometimes we have it and sometimes we don't. It just depends what we feel like. Ha ha." I quietly say, "I'm not joking."

Wrong Bag

The girl who checked me in did not ask me any questions about the luggage I was checking. As I was looking for luggage tags to fill out, before I knew it, she hands me my boarding pass with the baggage claim stubs attached. I look behind her and I see my suitcase AND my carry-on disappearing on the belt.

"NO-O-O-O!" I exclaimed. 'That's the wrong bag!' When I walked up to the counter, I just unloaded my luggage, placing the suitcase and matching carry-on on the weigh scale. I meant to place my garment bag as my second piece of checked luggage, not my carry-on. My carry-on had my $900. laptop in the front pocket. Unpadded, unprotected and uninsured. Oh, NO! We have to get that back. I am already rushed because I did not leave for the airport in time. Yes, my fault. I ask the Frontier staff at the counter how do we get my bag back? They kind of all say in unison some form of "No there's nothing that can be done." I think, that can't be possible. I'm certainly not the only person ever who mistakenly checked the wrong bag. There's got to be a way.

Where there's a Lead, there's No Way

I am a believer that there's always a way. Someone has the authority, the know-how, the whatever it takes, to fix a given problem. But my request was met with an attitude of ambivalence and lack of concern.

I ask, "How do we get my bag back? My laptop is in there. It will be destroyed."

A female Frontier staff member says, "You can't get it back. No one can. And yes, it may likely be destroyed. There's nothing that can be done."

My heart sinks. I have visions of retrieving my crushed, completely destroyed laptop upon arrival in Atlanta. I blurt out, "There must be something that can be done. Who's in charge?"

That same woman who was speaking hopelessness to me a moment ago, walks away from me, while emphatically stating, "I AM. I'm the Lead!"

Wow. She's the Lead?! The Lead of what? I felt no empathy whatsoever from this person who claimed to be in charge. What kind of customer service is that? Yes, again, I admit, I am the one who placed the wrong bag on the check-in scale. However, never once did the counter staff confirm with me that these are the bags I was checking. And regardless, if the customer makes a mistake, shouldn't the service professional do or at least attempt to do something to fix the problem?

As I stand there, frustrated and bewildered, I wonder what am I going to do? The clock is ticking. I need to retrieve that bag. My flight is scheduled to leave in about 30 minutes. I ask one of the other staff members if there is a supervisor or manager that we can contact.

This young woman replies, "Yes, she went to get the manager." What? The person who is the Lead, who gave me no hope or assurance walks away to go get the manager? How bizarre. She did not make any attempt to reassure me or tell that she was attempting to find a resolution. Rather, all she did was emphatically state, "Nothing can be done and NO One can get that bag back! It's GONE!"

She didn't say, "Just wait right here Mr. Weihman, I'll be right back." But now I'm told she went to go get the manager. So, maybe something *can* be done after all!

Maybe there is Hope

So, maybe something *can* be done after all!

Up to this point, I had not been impressed by the quality of care or concern by any of the Frontier staff members. Actually, I kind of felt as though they were being entertained by my plight.

Moments later, the supervisor, Sarah appears. I explain my situation, that I desperately need to retrieve the bag that was mistakenly checked. She assures me that she will do all she can to make this happen. Yay! Hooray. I finally feel that there is someone on my side. I am not relieved yet, but I am more hopeful than I was moments earlier. I ask if I should go to security and if she can just bring me the bag to security. She explains that the reason there is such a challenge with this situation is that once a bag is checked it can only go to one of two places; onto the plane or to baggage claim. If it goes to baggage claim, only the passenger is allowed to bring it to security.

She tells me to go downstairs to baggage claim, carousel 22 and wait for her to retrieve and send me the bag. She asks what my bag looks like and I describe it. It's black and white and has some designs on it. I really don't know how to describe it. My wife says it's white with black flowers. I really didn't know how to describe it well.

Here's a tip. When you travel, always take photos of all your luggage and have it saved on your phone. If you ever find yourself in a similar predicament you can easily just show the picture of your bags.

I head to baggage claim as Sarah heads to the inner belly of the plane or whereever the luggage for this flight happens to be at this time. I arrive at carousel 22. It's empty. No flights listed on the sign board. No people. No other baggage. That's good. I won't have to sort through other bags. Just wait for mine. So, I wait. And Wait. And Wait. Seemed like forever.

In reality it was a total of about 10 or 11 minutes. Even still, we are really cutting it close. I still have to go through security. It is now 12:09. Gates close at 12:40. I have barely 30 minutes to get my bag, get through security, ride the tram and get to my gate. Sarah is on my side. I know we'll make this happen. I'm confident, but I'm sweating.

I had texted my wife while I was still up at the counter hoping for some kind of remedy to retrieve my bag. My message to her was, 'I checked the wrong bag.'

She replied, "You're stressing me out." Probably shouldn't have sent her that message. So, to make her not feel stressed, while I was waiting for my bag at carousel 22 I prepared a pre-text. Once I got my bag, I would just hit send and she would feel better, knowing that all was well. My pre-text read: Got my bag. Now going to security.

As I'm standing at Carousel 22 waiting for my bag to arrive, suddenly another Frontier staff person appears and stands about 10-12 feet away from me, in front of the baggage carousel. She is texting on her phone, she looks over at me a couple times but does not engage me nor introduce herself to me. I think that's a bit odd. Finally, after a couple minutes, I walk over and approach her, introducing myself. She then responds, tells me her name, Maria (not her real name). Apparently, she is texting with Sarah and is there to ensure that I get my bag. She says to me, "Sarah, has your bag and is sending it now. She will escort you to security, once you get your bag." This sounds very promising to me. Sarah is going to 'escort' me to security. No problem. I'm very excited. Just waiting for my bag to appear.

I thank Maria for the information and then within a few seconds, at the top of the Carousel, out through the chute, here appears my bag! I am thrilled. It seems like forever for it to actually drop onto the belt and make its way toward me. Finally, there it is, on the belt in front of me. I grab it off the carousel. I don't remember if I smiled or said something to Maria. All I know is, I have my bag.

Wrong Bag- Again!

I head towards the elevator to meet Sarah upstairs to be escorted to security. I press 'Send' on the text for Michelle. This will ease her worries a bit. I take a couple steps and begin to run towards the elevator, when I realize something is not quite right. OH NO-O-O-O!!! I look down. It's the WRONG BAG! Sarah had sent my suitcase, not my carry-on!

I am stunned! I walk towards Maria and tell her the problem. Now, Sarah must go back and send the correct bag down to Carousel 22, AND they have to return the suitcase to be put back onto the airplane. I follow Maria into her office. She texts Sarah, telling her the situation. Then she makes a call, I presume to whomever is loading baggage onto the plane to inform them that there is one more still to come.

And then I wait. Again. I also realized that the text I sent my wife, "Got my bag, heading to security now." is incorrect. I decide not to stress her out more by informing her of the new status. I wait, staring at the Carousel 22. I'm praying that we can make it onto plane in time. I am thankful that Sarah is doing all she can to retrieve my bag. I'm frustrated, wondering how they could send the suitcase rather than the carry-on.

The time is ticking by and I still have to go thru security. Finally, the correct bag, my carry-on with my laptop in it, appears on the carousel. I thank Maria. I run to the elevator. I go up one flight to level 2 where I see Sarah in front of me with-I'm thinking a cart, something for us to ride to get to and through security quickly. No, instead, she is running and says to me, "Let's go." So, I run too. Here we are, running, Yes, I mean running, through the airport towards security.

When we get to security, she flashes her badge and I guess she assumed they would just let us pass through. No way. TSA does not care. You're late. Too bad. We did, however get to bypass the line. Thank God for that.

But now, I still had to go through the same, normal, time consuming procedure. Shoes, belt off, everything out of pockets, etc. Once I had placed all my items in the multiple bins, the TSA agent points to the other side of the aisle and tells me to take all my bins to that side, because this side is now closed. Ugh! Ok, so I do. I get through security, Sarah is waiting for me. I finish gathering my things and then we run, again. This time to the tram to ride to the gates.

We get on the tram and sit down. As we sat there facing each other, I say to Sarah, "I did not intend to create a lot of excitement for your team this morning." Sarah looks at me with a big grin on her face, (which I can't imagine why she would be so happy) and she says to me, "I always enjoy when someone presents me with a challenge, an obstacle to overcome and I get the opportunity to fix it." And that was about the extent of our conversation, I thanked her as the tram doors opened and we then proceed to run for the last time; to my gate. I ask Sarah for a quick picture. We take a selfie, I hug her and walk down the gangway to board my plane- 5 minutes after gates were scheduled to close.

As I boarded the plane, I was expecting the passengers all to applaud or to say something, either happy for me or perhaps annoyed that I was the one who delayed the plane taking off. No, nothing like that happened. They all, perhaps including the flight crew, were entirely unaware of what had just transpired over the past 42 minutes. The flight attendant greeted me and asked me to quickly take my seat. I found my seat and let out a huge sigh of relief.

I was on my way to Atlanta to speak at the National Customer Service Association Conference. I immediately knew that this experience I just had would inform my presentation entitled, "The Customer Experience". Sarah truly embodies what being your customer's hero is all about. Thank you, Sarah!

The above story is a great example of how one person can either positively or negatively affect the Customer Experience. Every day we have, as Shep Hyken calls it, the 'Awesome Responsibility' to make a difference in a customer or client's life. It is rarely a grand heroic feat, rather, it is more often, the small gestures that show the customer that you care. It is the way we greet them and treat them. It's in how we send out positive, caring energy to them. It is in the smile that shines and sends a message that is more powerful than words. It is in how we embrace this responsibility and engage the wonderful people who come into our space, cross our path and become not only customers, but as my wife, Michelle, likes to say, 'a part of the story'.

It is my intention, my hope, and my desire, that as you read *The Customer Experience*, you will feel inspired to elevate the service that you provide your customers. As an author, I recognize that my customer is you, the one reading this book. I pray that you find joy in these pages as you consider how you might lead your team to greater levels of service to your customers. I invite you to read these pages with an open mind and an open heart. The principles and ideas that resonate with you, take them, use them, implement them. The ones that do not speak to you, leave them on the pages for someone else to come along and find.

I am humbled and grateful that you have come into my space and you now hold in your hands a powerful book that has the potential to dramatically and positively impact the way you impact your customers.

As you engage these pages, make yourself comfortable, set an intention for yourself to discover at least one golden nugget of value from each chapter.

Each and every time you sit down with *The Customer Experience*, may you feel excited for and open to what inspiration is coming to you now.

May the words on these pages bring a smile to your face, a positive expectancy in your mind and a feeling of joy and confidence in your heart.

You, my Friend, Dear Reader, are now a part of my story, and I, a part of yours. Joyful reading to you.

In Service,
Christoff J. Weihman
Las Vegas, Nevada 2018

Chapter 1

ENERGY & EMOTION

"It's (we're) all energy; it's (we're) all connected; it all comes back to you."

Flushers-Original Screenplay
by Christoff J. Weihman

Thoughts are Things

I first began to think about the topic of Energy and Emotion when I happened upon Napoleon Hill's classic, *Think and Grow Rich* about 20 years ago. In the very first chapter entitled, 'Thoughts are Things', he states, "Truly, thoughts are things, and powerful things at that."

Thoughts are things. What kind of things are they? They are electrical impulses that carry within them great potential. Our thoughts actually emit energy. Our thoughts influence and even create emotion within us. Science has taught us that all living beings and systems are made up of vibrating and spinning molecules. That includes us as human beings. Another way to state that is that we are vibrational beings.

Our thoughts are things and they emit energy. We, ourselves are energetic beings. We are made up of energy. We have the ability to influence our own frequency or energy level. I know you know what I'm talking about. If you do, we use the term *resonate*. Does what I'm sharing resonate with you?

We've all experienced one of those days when we just weren't feeling it. We felt that our energy tank was on low or even very close to empty. Nothing specifically bad happened to us. We weren't necessarily sick-we just didn't feel right. We were lethargic, no zest for life, no vibrancy in our voice, no skip in our step-just low energy. Yet, even though we felt this way, we decided to make a change, to pull it together, muster up the strength and go to work, or to that meeting we had been dreading, or whatever it was that we had to do but didn't feel like doing. We did it. We changed our thoughts, made a decision to act and we were able to elevate our own energy level. We raised our vibration.

Human Energy Generators

I love what Brendon Burchard says in his inspirational book, *The Charge*. In it he states, "The power plant doesn't have energy. It generates energy.' Think about that. We can say, "I don't have energy." But then we can make a decision to do something about it, to make a change. We are our own energy generator. We are human power plants.

Our energy, our thoughts and emotions are inextricably linked together. We are imbued by our Creator with an extraordinary gift, which is the ability to control our thoughts, affect our own emotions and raise or lower our energy level.

So, you may be wondering and thinking to yourself right now, "What does all of this have to do with the 'Customer Experience?" My answer is...EVERYTHING! That is why even though, originally this chapter on Energy & Emotion was meant to be chapter 9-for that is where it came in the progression of the chapters, I am so convinced that this is the core of what *The Customer Experience* is about that I decided this *must* be Chapter 1. Understanding the power and potential of Energy & Emotion is the foundation, the very core of everything else that follows.

One more point I must share with you before we discuss specifically how Energy & Emotion affect the Customer Experience. Not only are we all blessed with the wonderful gift of being able to control our thoughts and emotions, and being able to raise our vibration, we also are gifted to be able to connect with other human beings using these three faculties-our thoughts, emotions and energy. And we have the potential to either positively or negatively affect those with whom we interact.

Serving our customers is much deeper than just relating to them on a surface or superficial level. Although that may be what a lot of customer service is focused upon, my intention for *The Customer Experience* is for us to discuss and discover together, how to truly connect with our customers on a deeper level.

The Emotional Journey

Every time a customer interacts with you, your team or your business in any way, that person embarks upon an emotional journey. Depending upon the type of business and the service being provided, that emotional journey may last but a few seconds-as in the case of a patron walking into a gas station to purchase gas. This is really just a quick trip-sorry, yes, a pun. While in other situations, such as planning a wedding, or purchasing a home, the emotional journey may last as long as several months or more.

A customer's experience of shopping at a big box retail store may take place over an hour or more, whereas dinner with your spouse and friends out on the town, may last for several hours. If your business is one in which there is more of a long-term interaction with your clients, such as therapists, attorneys or real estate agents, that emotional journey may last for a period of months or even years. Although each of the above-mentioned experiences is different from the next, regardless of the type of service you offer-that interaction between you and your customer is an emotional journey. In every instance, you as the Service Professional have a powerful ability to positively, or negatively, influence how that interaction and experience will play out.

So, what exactly do I mean by an emotional journey? Whenever a customer walks into, calls into, or connects with your place of business, they have a specific emotional state or to borrow a term from, Esther Hicks, author of *Ask and It Is Given*, an 'emotional set point'. This is the starting point of what they are feeling at the beginning of their interaction or experience with you. Of course, for each person, and every situation and customer experience it will be different.

For some, their emotional set point may be a positive one-when they're going out for a celebration dinner. For others, it may not be a positive emotional set point, perhaps when a loved one has died and they must call or visit a funeral home to make funeral arrangements. That person is not going to be in an upbeat positive emotional state. This person's emotional set point is going to be one of sadness, feeling somber and a great sense of loss. Each situation provides an opportunity for you as the Service Professional to positively or negatively affect the customer's emotional set point. Their emotional journey may be elevated by you or not.

Touch Points

During many customer experiences, there is often more than one team member who interacts with the customer. Each interaction with the customer, whether by the same or various team members, is called a 'touchpoint'. "Touchpoints," according to Jeff Tobe, author of *Coloring Outside the Lines,* "are opportunities to make a positive impact upon the customer and to enhance their experience."

Let's diagram a hypothetical emotional journey with multiple touchpoints and see what it looks like.

My wife, Michelle and I are going out for dinner to celebrate our anniversary. Our emotional set point is a feeling of happiness, romance and celebration. Perhaps we have a bit of positive expectation mixed in as well.

We have reservations at one of our favorite restaurants here in Las Vegas. Rather than driving, we decide to take a Lyft to the restaurant. We are both looking forward to a great dinner and celebrating together. We are dressed to the nines. Our Lyft arrives in a timely manner and pulls up in front of our home. The driver gets out of his car, introduces himself to us (his name is Andrew) and proceeds to open the doors for us. Touchpoint # 1.

We get in the car, and after confirming our destination with us, Andrew comments on how decked out we are and asks what the occasion is. We tell him that it's our anniversary and the conversation is upbeat and positive. He shows genuine interest and seems to enjoy as we tell him our story of how we met, of moving to Las Vegas and about our three puppies. Touchpoint # 2

We arrive at our destination and we are feeling quite positive because of the wonderful start to our evening. Something so simple as a nice and courteous Lyft driver, and friendly conversation created a great experience for us, rather than merely driving us to a destination.

We walk up to the restaurant and immediately two staff members open the double doors for us to enter as they greet us almost in unison. "Hi, Good Evening. Welcome."

Michelle and I smile at each other, thanking the staff members as we enter the restaurant. Touchpoint # 3

We approach the host stand and wait to be greeted. The hostess is looking frantic and stressed. There are about a dozen other diners waiting to be seated. It is a very busy evening at this classy restaurant. After a couple minutes, finally, the hostess looks up at us and says, "Name?"

No "Hello". No "Good evening" and certainly no "Welcome, do you have a reservation?" She simply says, "Name?"

I tell her our name as she is now staring back down on the reservation book or system or whatever. Without even looking up, she says, "It'll be 45 minutes." Touchpoint # 4

Hmm. Forty-five minutes, I think. That doesn't seem right. We do have a reservation. I mention about the reservation. She looks up and then back down again. By now other hostesses join her at the stand. They're all looking down, mumbling to each other. After some minutes, a manager, I presume, comes over. The hostess says something quietly to him. He then says, "Weihman…okay, we'll seat you now. Follow me."

He doesn't apologize, he doesn't explain the confusion, nor does he introduce himself. He merely escorts us to our table and hands us each a menu. Touchpoint # 5

As we're sitting at our table, waiting for a server to arrive, an older gentleman-the server assistant, approaches. He greets us with "Good evening. Welcome." We respond in kind. He then says, "You both look so nice this evening. What are you celebrating?" Touchpoint # 6

He offers to pour water. We request bottled water and he smiles and says, "I'll get that right out to you. Marcus is your server, he'll be out in a few minutes. I'm Sergio and I'm his assistant."

Now, I won't go on to describe the entire experience that evening but consider that within a very short time there were 5 Touchpoints at the restaurant. Six touchpoints on our Customer Journey up to this point if we include the Lyft driver. I'm sure if you imagine yourself in our shoes, that you can easily feel the range of emotions we were experiencing at that time. Remember, our emotional set point was one of happiness, celebration and romance. The Lyft driver certainly met us at that point and enhanced that feeling by asking what we were celebrating and engaging us in upbeat conversation. The greeters at the restaurant entrance with their warm, friendly greeting added a feeling of welcome.

Then, suddenly when we reached the host stand that elevated emotion took a nose dive with the unfriendly behavior of the hostess. The manager who seated us didn't do anything to bring us back up. But once we met and were engaged by Sergio, we were again hopeful that the evening was back on track.

I do realize that most people don't think of their business in this manner, analyzing and dissecting each point of interaction with the customer. It may not be natural for many Service Professionals to view their interaction with their customers in this way. And that is precisely the point of *The Customer Experience*-to inspire and encourage us to open our eyes and view the Customer Experience in a new light.

Our experience described above is a very common and simple example, but this Emotional Journey of which I speak, plays out thousands of times a day in companies, organizations and businesses all across the world in every industry.

If you deal with, interact with, serve, sell to, communicate with or provide a product to customers-you are involved in the Customer Experience. Each time you or your team member interacts with a customer, you possess the potential, to powerfully impact that customer's experience-either positively or negatively. In the past it may not be something that you or your team had been aware of. Even people who *give good service,* up to this point, may not have been aware of the Emotional Journey of the Customer. We'll talk more in depth in Chapter 9 -Energy and Emotion (Part 2) about how our Energy and Emotion affects and influences our interaction with our customers.

Customer Feeling Chart

Type of Business/ Place	Emotional Set Point	Desired Feeling/ Outcome
Law Office	Anxiety/Uninformed	Trust/Hopeful
Dental Office	Fear/ Self-conscious	Calm/Peace
Church (First time visitor)	Self-conscious/ uncomfortable	Welcome/Accepted
Seminar	Excitement/ Apprehension	Trust/ Positivity
Hospital	Worry/ Fear/ Uncertainty	Cared for/ Heard/ Hopeful
Car Dealership	Excitement/Distrust	Trust/ Happiness
Restaurant (on a Date)	Anticipation/Romance	Welcome/Relaxed/ Engaged
Hotel	Tired from Travel/ Anxious	Welcome/Stress-free
Cruise ship	Excited/Nervous/ Fearful	Welcome/Cared for/ Relaxed

It is important to be aware of what are the feelings that your customers feel when they come into or engage your place of business (their emotional set point or starting point) and what are the feelings or mood you want to create for them/ desired outcome.

Three things to consider and be aware/conscious, cognizant of relating to your customer's feelings/mood:

1. The feeling/emotion before or when they walk into your business. (Emotional Set Point)
2. What their desired outcome is/Your desired outcome for them.
3. What feeling/mood they are leaving with.

Consider this; in every customer interaction the desired outcome or end result is always a positive feeling. Do you agree? If you leave the customer with a positive and elevated feeling, then in a meaningful way you have contributed to their overall customer experience.

What are some of the touchpoints in your interaction with your clientele?

Are there any changes you might like to make to how these touchpoints are carried out?

When you positively affect how your customers feel, how does that make you feel?

How often are you aware of your customer's emotional set point?

How often do you think you positively affect their emotional set point?

What steps might you consider taking to elevate your customers' experience?

Chapter 2

ENVISIONMENT

"Start before the beginning"
Christoff J. Weihman

H ave you ever wondered what it would be like if all your customers loved what you do for them? Have you ever imagined how it would be if you had the perfect team, delivering amazing customer service, on a consistent basis to your appreciative, valued customers? And what would it be like if your business was booming because the experience your customers have when they engage your business was above and beyond anything that they could experience elsewhere? I want to tell you that all of that is possible. But first you must envision it.

A foundational character trait of all great leaders is the ability to see beyond what is visible on the surface. The Bible tells us that "Without vision, the people perish." In business, without vision, the people will flounder and have no clear direction. They'll wonder why they're doing what they're doing. They'll get stuck in the minutiae and never grow and flourish and they will not have a powerful positive impact on their customers, let alone upon the community. Vision is vital to the success of any organization.

In order to 'Consciously Create and Elevate the Emotional Journey' in which we are engaged, we as leaders, business owners and directors of organizations must be visionaries. We must learn to become masters of Envisionment. All of the great leaders of the past have been. Consider Henry Ford, Thomas Edison, the Wright Brothers and Walt Disney. All of them titans and pioneers in their respective industries. Actually, they were much more than that. They were creators-inventors and trailblazers of their specific industries.

Walt Disney

Walt Disney was not a superior cartoonist, in fact he wasn't even the one who drew Mickey Mouse. But that didn't matter. He had the vision for it. He envisioned the character and two other animators drew Mickey. First, Hugh Harman did a few rough sketches of Walt's idea of an anthropomorphic mouse. Next, Ubi Werks took those ideas as inspiration to create Mickey Mouse. However, it was really Walt Disney who created the character and is credited with Mickey's creation. His thoughts became things. He not only envisioned a cast of memorable characters, but ultimately, he built a kingdom around them-The Magic Kingdom. And that kingdom which sprung forth with an idea of a mouse character is today worldwide and worth billions of dollars.

Walt Disney had envisionment. Do you? Of course, he had naysayers. I'm imagining that his parents and peers didn't fathom a lucrative future for him coming from his imagination and doodles. But he envisioned something that others could not yet see. It was that vision that gave him his drive, his perseverance and his quest for more.

The Wright Brothers

Likewise, we could tell a similar story of Orville and Wilbur Wright and their vision of a manned flying machine. Who were they to imagine such a ludicrous idea? They merely owned a bicycle repair shop. But they had envisionment. They believed the impossible, what had not yet been done, could be done. Anything is possible. And they let that vision guide them to success. Their envisionment has affected the lives of billions of people over the past 100 years.

The Envisionment of Steve Jobs

And what of Steve Jobs of Apple and his powers of Envisionment? What he created with ipods, ipads and the iphone has touched and changed the lives of millions and millions of people around the world. But did Steve Jobs actually create the iphone or the ipod? Again, the answer is technically no. But without his envisionment-most likely, these devices never would have come into being.

The Customer Experience begins with Envisionment

So where does Envisionment find its role or its place in regards to the Customer Experience? We must imagine and determine a clear picture of what kind of experience we wish to create and deliver for our customers. Is it to be fun? Is it for them to feel cared for? Is it to be an experience that is exciting, engaging, romantic, exhilarating? Will what you offer be peaceful and relaxing, or uplifting and inspiring? Each one is different. You must determine what is the experience that you wish to create for your customers.

It is quite revealing that, when asked, many business owners or leaders don't actually know what type of Customer Experience they are aspiring to provide for their clientele. At our EXCELLERATE SERVICE Seminars, we have an exercise which we guide our participants through that helps them discover the answer to that question. It is nearly impossible to successfully implement and deliver a five-star customer service experience, if we don't know what that looks like or feels like from the very beginning. To say you aspire to give five-star service is great, but without clarity on what type of experience, we are still missing the mark.

Every industry is different and every business within each industry may have a different type of experience they are aspiring to give to their clientele. The experience I expect from a resort hotel will be different from what I expect at an Urgent care facility, which will be different from what I would experience at a carwash. As leaders and Service Professionals we must be conscious and cognizant and have clarity of the vision of the type of Customer Experience we seek to provide.

Peter Anthony

Before I even began contemplating writing *The Customer Experience*, I was unconsciously doing research for it. One person who taught me a great deal about the Customer Journey and the role of emotions is my good friend and mentor Peter Anthony Wynn. Peter Anthony is the Founder and CEO of YouWillChangetheWorld.com -an online course creation company that assembles the best and the brightest speakers, instructors and educators, from a myriad of industries and disciplines from around the world. Peter Anthony and his team help them get their message/ their genius out to the world.

When Peter Anthony and I met he was transitioning from a 20 plus year career as an award-winning hairdresser in New York, to becoming a mentor of speakers and entrepreneurs in Las Vegas. When he speaks he draws many of his examples from those 20 plus years of being a hairdresser in New York. I've learned many things about success in business from Peter Anthony, but the one thing that has made the greatest impact on me is how he was able to create a name and brand for himself in a sea of other high-end hairdressers in New York.

He said he mastered the art of making his clientele feel good. (my paraphrase). I wasn't sure what he meant at first. He then explained.

There's a lot of great, super talented hairdressers. So how did he set himself apart? When he would consult with a client, while they are seated in his chair and he is observing their current hair style, he wouldn't ask them what style or shape or type of cut they wanted. Nope. Instead, he would ask them one very simple, yet profound question, "How do you want to feel from this cut?"

How do you want to feel?! Crazy, isn't it? The truth is, it's brilliant. He understood that if he could tap into what was the driving force behind this person coming to sit in his chair and pay his high fees, and he was able to make them feel the way they wanted to-then he had them. Loyal, raving fan.

A short time right before Peter Anthony finally closed his salon in Las Vegas, he told me to bring my wife, Michelle in for a complimentary cut. And I witnessed him do exactly what he said he had done throughout his career. Michelle sat in his chair and he didn't ask how she wanted it cut, he asked, "How do you want to feel?" Of course, the answer is different for everyone. Some women when they get their hair done want to feel playful, others want to feel powerful, others want to feel sexy.

As Service Professionals, we cannot necessarily directly ask our customers, "How do you want to feel after our interaction?". That is why having a clear vision is foundational.

If you're starting from scratch, you have a huge advantage. If, however, you're a leader and you've inherited a team or group by virtue of a promotion, or you've been newly hired into your position, there may be entrenched mindsets and behaviors that will need to be changed, modified or flat out done away with. Realize this, if you were hired into or promoted into that position, you were put there for a reason. Therefore, you, too, must have a clear vision for the type of experience you are aspiring to create for your customers.

Envision Your A-Team
You Attract Who You Are

Once you've clarified the type of experience you are creating for your customers, now you must determine what kind of team you want to attract. What are the core values that you want them to resonate with? If you put this forth from the beginning, then there's a lesser chance of attracting people who are not in alignment with your core values and a greater chance of people coming into your organization who are of the same mindset and heart-set.

So, it is here that we must start, before the beginning. We must envision not only the type of experience we wish to create and deliver to our future clientele, but also, we must determine what type of person will be best to help execute our vision? Long before you open the doors of your business; before you hire your graphic artist to create your eye-catching, stunning logo; before you begin any social media campaign, you must answer these questions.

What type of company do you want to be? How will you separate yourself/your company from the marketplace? What type of experience will your customers have when they interact with you? As mentioned above, even if you are coming into an already existing business, you still must know the answers to these questions. If we don't clarify the type of experience we want our customers to receive, then how could we ever ensure what they experience?

Start before the beginning. Determine in your mind and with your leadership team, what is the outcome you want to achieve? This will then enable you to better determine the qualities you desire in your team. It's not merely about filling positions. We'll discuss this in more detail in the next chapter on Employment.

"Good business leaders create a vision, articulate the vision, passionately own the vision and relentlessly drive it to completion" Jack Welch, former CEO of GE.

To envision is to imagine with an unshackled mind that is unhindered and not influenced by up-to-this-date current reality.

We must think big. Believe big. Just because it's never been done should never be a reason to believe that it cannot be done. Businesses often don't deliver exceptional customer experiences for their clientele because they haven't spent enough time envisioning. So much time, effort and planning are put into the type of floor tiles that are going to be laid, the color of paint on the walls and all the other physical aspects of the business and also into the physical product to be sold. But what amount of time and creative imagination are you and your leadership team investing into crafting an amazing experience for your customers?

My wife, Michelle is a nurse at one of the major hospitals in Las Vegas. We recently heard from another nurse friend of hers who told us of a recent training she attended at the hospital where she works in Los Angeles. The customer service trainer had as a stated goal: "to make the hospital experience more like a trip to Disneyland."

While Disneyland is known to be the "happiest place on earth", and yes, hospitals could up their happiness quotient, attempting to translate that to a hospital environment, is incongruent. Yes, it is cutting edge and thoughtful to think outside the box and be creative, but equating a hospital stay with a trip to Disneyland makes no sense. Certainly, there are many ways to make a hospital more friendly and more welcoming, but it must be appropriate to the specific industry and resonate with your clientele.

Communicate Your Vision

The office supply store giant, Staples clearly states one of their visions of the customer experience they provide, is to make it *Easy* for the customer. They even have an *Easy* button. I personally have never shopped nor done business at a Staples, so, I cannot attest to whether it translates to the customer experience, but I would expect that it does. And friends who do use them, tell me that indeed it is EASY.

Many companies are successful in articulating their vision in a catchy slogan that is simple, memorable and creates a good or positive feeling in the customer when they hear it, say it or see it.

"Like a good neighbor, State Farm is there." -Communicates a feeling of security and help in time of need.

"When it absolutely has to be there overnight." Fedex- Communicates dependability.

"Fly the friendly skies." United Airlines – Communicates-Friendly, Accommodating service

Clearly articulating the type and quality of service experience you provide is important. However, just having a catchy, memorable slogan doesn't guarantee that a great customer experience is the outcome. Why? Because you must have the right team to deliver on that promise to your customers. Great Customer Experiences are designed and orchestrated by a Great Customer Service Team.

Are you ready to begin attracting you're A-Team? If so, let's move on to Chapter 3.

Chapter 3

EMPLOYMENT

> *"Do great things and those who want to do great things will find you and want to work with you."*
>
> Grant Cardone
> *Be Obsessed or Be Average*

Attracting & Assembling Your A-Team

Once you've envisioned the type of customer experience you intend to create and deliver *to* and *for* your customers, next, you need a Team. But not just any team. You need a Team that:

1. Understands and gets your vision
2. Resonates with the vision and desires to align themselves with it
3. Is a right fit and wants to serve and contribute value to the Team

It's not just a matter of saying, "What positions do we need to fill?" and then going about putting out ads to fill them. Employment must be of a higher mindset.

> *Our goal must be to attract to ourselves like-minded individuals who embrace our vision, embody our values and are an extension of our mindset, energy and spirit.*

If you want a Team that does more than just fill roles or hold positions, or fulfill the job descriptions, then it is vital that your approach from the very beginning be different than what is typical. You are desiring to find individuals that are right for your Team, and who will help create and perpetuate the great culture you've envisioned.

Attracting and assembling your A-Team is not easy, but when done correctly, with the right foresight and in the right attitude, you will be happy with the results. There are many factors to consider when attracting and hiring for your Team.

It goes without saying, but I will say it anyway, no plan, or formula is 100% foolproof. Meaning, that no matter how much you screen and no matter how diligent or disciplined you and your leadership team are in this process, some bad eggs will inevitably slip through. You will hire the wrong person or at least not the best person sometimes. Recognize it, accept it and deal with it when the time comes and don't beat yourself up over it.

It is important to remember that the people you do bring onboard must resonate with your organization's vision and core values.

Recently, when I spoke at the National Customer Service Association's (NCSA) national conference in Atlanta, I had the privilege of listening to Mark Moraitakis of Chick-Fil-A, speak. He talked about the importance of clearly stating the company's vision and values to prospective applicants. He says this accomplishes two things. First, it tends to attract like-minded and like-hearted (my paraphrase) individuals, who will apply for the positions you are seeking team members for. The second thing it does is it filters out those that are not in alignment with the stated vision.

For example, Chick-Fil-A's stated mission is:

"To glorify God by being a faithful steward of all that is entrusted to us, and to be a positive influence to all who come into contact with Chick-Fil-A."

This is not something that the company just springs on someone once they've been hired. Instead, it's put forth in the information they share with new candidates *before* they are hired. From the above mission statement, it would be reasonable that applicants should at least feel comfortable around a faith-focused team of leaders and staff. And those with obvious negative attitude, energy and outlook on life will probably not feel comfortable to even apply to work at this company.

Does having a clear mission statement and vision and communicating that to applicants guarantee 100% that someone who doesn't resonate won't get hired? No, as I stated earlier, nothing is completely foolproof. People who are seeking employment are very clever and creative. They can pretend, they can do research, and they can act during the interview process, but even if they do slip through and get hired, eventually they will be found out. Their deceit will ultimately shine through and not in a positive way.

If an individual gets hired who does not truly resonate with the company's mission and vision, one of two things will inevitably happen. First, that individual will most likely self-select themselves to move on. They will quit or create a situation that will force them to be let go.

The other and less likely scenario, would be that they will allow themselves to be positively influenced by the culture that originally, they did not ascribe to or resonate with. They will slowly change their mindset, their attitude and then their actions will follow. The "If you can't beat'em, join'em" phenomenon will kick in. I have seen this happen and heard stories of this taking place. However, I would advise you to not expect it. So, don't hold your breath.

I know of one example at a company where there was a certain culture that became entrenched from years of lack of accountability and weak leadership. Many of the staff who had seniority, were allowed to slack off on certain requirements, they were not disciplined or reprimanded, nor were they held accountable for their mistakes. They were held in such high esteem by their peers and management, merely because of their tenure with the company. This is a very dangerous situation for the health of any organization. Yes, it is good in part, to reward someone for their dedication and years of service to a company or organization. However, to overlook ineptness because we don't want to hurt the feelings of a senior staff person is very unwise. And as I've stated elsewhere, just because someone has been doing a job a certain way for a number of years, does not ensure that they are doing it correctly. I learned long ago, that contrary to popular belief, practice *does not* make perfect. Only if the way one is practicing is right or correct, will it lead to or approach the orbit of perfection.

The correct statement is: "Perfect practice, makes perfect"

In the above example I mentioned, something interesting happened. The leadership left and new management came in. When this happened, the staff, who were accustomed to being allowed free reign with little accountability, began to feel challenged and threatened. At the very least, some were feeling uncomfortable and unsure of what these new changes would bring.

So, what happened as the new leadership began to implement changes, raise standards and require accountability for *all* the staff? Some decided they would do better elsewhere, and they actually followed the old leaders to their new assignment at a different company. Others, struggled and resisted at first. But eventually, they realized that the new management truly had their best interest and the interests of the customers at heart.

In the end, those that stayed embraced the changes and began to excel in their roles unlike never before. As a result, during the first 2 years of the new leadership being in place, the company and this one department in particular, received multiple awards for customer service excellence, and customer satisfaction in a number of different categories. The overall culture of the entire company changed by what began with new leadership with a right vision coming into lead one department.

Perfect on Paper, but...

I am a lifelong learner and my teachers are all around me. I seek out and welcome input from, and am influenced by many thought leaders, some well-known, others not so well known. Regardless of the source, I respect all of them and their input and expertise.

By now, it should be quite evident to you that one person whom I am constantly learning from is my wife, Michelle. She is a supervisor of the Intensive Care Unit of a major, very busy hospital in Las Vegas. Daily, she is in the trenches, constantly being met with challenges and opportunities to create positive experiences for her patients and their families. All the while, she is always being conscious of the experience her nursing team is having. She is very well aware of the fact that her team members are as much her customers, as are the patients lying in the beds.

The mission of the hospital where she works is: 'Patient and Family centered care'. That means, that unlike many hospitals, this hospital has no set visiting hours. Patient's family members are free to visit their loved ones, any time, day or night. No time restrictions.

She recounted to me a time when she was interviewing potential candidates to join their nursing team. She asked, as she always does, a very qualified, very experienced, and highly recommended nurse what her view of 'Patient and families first' was. Her response really shocked

Michelle. The candidate's reply was, "Family members have no place at a hospital. That's why I only work night shift. I can take care of my patients properly without dealing with or worrying about family members. All they do is get in the way."

The candidate had almost a look of horror on her face when Michelle explained the open visiting hours policy to her. Needless to say, while this candidate was extremely qualified and looked great on paper, she was not a right fit. She was not a good candidate to play on Michelle's team.

I like what bestselling author, speaker and sales guru, Grant Cardone says in his book, *Be Obsessed or Be Average*; "You want people on your team who will do anything for you; jump off buildings, run through walls, and believe they can fly because of you."

Recruiters

Some companies choose to use outside recruiters or a staffing agency to assist them in filling positions. This can be very helpful, time saving and convenient. However, I'd like to offer a word of advice. I worked for a few years in the staffing industry in 2 different states and I was frankly, a bit surprised to discover what sometimes transpires.

Companies will gladly pay hefty commissions to recruiters to do the heavy lifting so, to speak. The recruiters find the candidates, do the background checks, employment verifications, and set up the interviews with the hiring company. But be wary. It is still important that you also check and confirm that the information that is being supplied to you about the candidate is true and accurate.

Recent statistics show that up to 80% of all applicants, across the board, regardless of industry, have false or exaggerated information on their applications and resumes. I know that may seem staggering and unbelievable, but I can attest first hand, from working in the staffing industry myself, that this does happen. I worked at a company, a well-known staffing agency, that did temporary assignment, contract and permanent placement. My job was business development, to go out and get the accounts. I represented the staffing/recruiting company to the business community.

One of the most important checks to be done in recruiting is an employment verification-to confirm that this applicant did in fact, work at said company, in such position, with these responsibilities, for a stated period of time. I assumed since this was our process, that that is what was being done. I came to find out later that almost 90% of the candidates that we were presenting for positions never had an employment verification done on them by my colleagues!

Sometimes a staffing or recruiting company may neglect to do an employment verification, and sometimes a candidate may lie on their resume. It is incumbent upon you, whomever is doing the hiring, to ask. Don't assume that what you see on paper is accurate. Ask, and I guarantee the truth will eventually come out. The one area that is the most common where candidates tend to embellish the truth is the scope of responsibilities that they had at their previous job.

Recruiters can be a great asset. Be aware and tell them what you expect. After all, this is your A-Team you are assembling.

You may be thinking that what is on a person's resume is not nearly as important as what they present of themselves in person. The person is more important than what's on paper. However, both are of equal importance. You don't want to attract people who are good hearted, positive minded, nice individuals who are incompetent and cannot do the job well. On the other hand, no one wants someone on their team that is highly qualified and very experienced, but who is impossible to work with because of their attitude.

4 Pillars of WOW! Customer Service

1. **Internal Components**
2. **Skills, Techniques & Knowledge**
3. **Customer-centric Mentality**
4. **Creating a Culture of WOW!**

When considering whom to bring on board your Team, it is crucial to understand the 4 Pillars of WOW! and find people who embody them. These will be discussed in the next chapter.

But first, Pillar number 1, Internal Components, must be present in the candidates you are considering to bring onto your team.

As important as the other 3 Pillars are, in order to be successful in creating a cohesive team to carry out your vision of how you want your customers/clientele to be served, your team must possess the Internal Components.

Inside Over Outside

In my first book, *Getting to WOW!*, the first five chapters focus on the Internal Components that are vital to customer service excellence. For a full in-depth description of them, I recommend you pick up a copy of *Getting to WOW!* Below is a brief overview of the 5 Internal Components.

The Internal Components

1. **Mindset, Attitude, Positive Energy (MAP)**

    Having the right mindset, attitude and positive energy is not only a foundational internal component, it also must permeate everything we do. The core essence of *The Customer Experience,* revolves around the understanding that our mind, emotions and energy always have an impact upon our interaction with our customers. Once we understand that and embrace it, then we can consciously determine how we are showing up daily with our customers. What kind of energy are you sending out? What feelings are you helping create for your clients? How are you positively or negatively affecting their emotional journey? We will cover this in greater detail in Chapter 9- Energy and Emotion.

For now, it's important that you as a leader, or hiring manager, be mindful of this internal component as you consider each applicant or potential Team member. Does this person lead with a positive attitude-do they see the opportunities or do they focus on the problems? A person with a perpetual negative attitude will not help lead your Team to success, regardless of how amazingly talented or skilled they may be.

2. **Passion**

The definition of Passion is what one is willing to suffer for- to sacrifice. When we speak of passion we're talking about a deep desire for something. Plain and simple the people you attract to your Team must have a passion for what your business or company stands for. We see it all too often today, even in the service industry where a person clearly doesn't want to be doing what they're doing. They're just going through the motions, following a checklist of steps to be performed. This is the nurse who doesn't actually do anything wrong in her care of the patient, but every engagement, every interaction, is done in a matter of fact manner. There's no heart-no passion.

It's the real estate agent that walks you through the house they're showing. He doesn't do anything incorrectly, but he has no excitement as he shows the house. That is all he's doing, showing the house. Here's the kitchen, here's the living room, there's the master bedroom. This person does not love what they do. Clearly, they only love the commission check. They never paint a picture or help create a vision for the client as they move through the house. They have no passion.

You must find people that have passion when assembling your team, for without passion there is no driving force. When you hire people that have no passion they will weigh down the rest of your team. And if they have no passion, a negative attitude typically goes hand in hand with that. They will only do the bare minimum of what's required of them. They'll always focus on the task and not the customer's outcome. They will do their duty and that is all. You must find people who have passion, even if they are less experienced and less skilled. Their passion will drive them to want to learn more, and they'll strive for excellence.

If you, as a leader, openly share your passion with your team it will ignite a spark within them. As I stated in *Getting to WOW!*, "Passion cannot be taught, nor bought. But it can be caught."

Share your vision and your passion with your team or potential team members, and the right ones will catch it. It may be but a faint flicker at first, but as long as the smallest ember of passion is within them, it can and will grow. Those that show up or join the team who don't have it won't be able to play along or pretend fo very long.

3. **Servant Heart**

Having a Servant Heart means serving because you enjoy it, gain pleasure from giving to others, because at the very core of

'Serving' is 'Giving'. When you serve, you give of your time, effort, energy, gifts, talents, skills, and emotions to others. To have a Servant Heart is to put the other person's needs above your own. You cannot be an effective service professional without this key component. If you are doing your job, merely because that is what you are supposed to do, if you are performing your role devoid of a Servant Heart, then you are not being true and authentic.

Having a Servant Heart does not mean having false humility. Nor does it mean to think lowly of yourself. On the contrary, those who have a Servant Heart, actually are ones who can and do exert great influence upon their customers, their clientele. When you approach Customer Service from the mindset and heart-set of truly wanting to serve, you will have a dramatic and positive effect upon your customers.

One can always tell when someone truly has a Servant Heart- they exude cheerfulness and joy. They radiate a warmth, an openness and a willingness to serve. They are filled with positivity and their demeanor is infectious. They are humble but confident. They know that they've been blessed for the purpose to be a blessing to others.

4. **Personal Pride**

This internal component is easily evident if an individual possesses it or not. It shows up in the way that they show up. Are they on time? Are they dressed for success? Do they carry themselves with assuredness and confidence?

Having a sense of Personal Pride is shown in one's work ethic. Do they give their all and strive to be the best they can be? Do they approach each task or assignment with the will and desire to do well or to just get the job done?

Personal Pride is simply stated in the phrase, "How you do anything is how you do everything." The team member who plays the position assigned to them with vigor and wholeheartedness, even though they were hoping for another position, is the type of team member you want to keep.

A person that does not have Personal Pride, cannot and will not show pride in the work they do. They will find and take short cuts. They will not follow protocol and procedures. Personal Pride is a crucial internal component, for without it you will have a team of independent-do-it-my-own-way mavericks. That will not lead to an A team. And it certainly won't result in your team delivering the best customer experience for your clientele.

5. **A Commitment to Excellence**

This internal component is very closely related to Personal Pride. One who has is committed to excellence is not satisfied with mediocrity. They are not of the mindset of 'its just good enough'. Being average is unacceptable to them.

A Commitment to Excellence starts in the mind, knowing that you have gifts to share and that in all things you should aspire to do your best. A person of Excellence is always a person of excellence. This is about integrity, giving one's all, all the time, every time. The person of Excellence sets the tone for the rest and leads not by words, but by the actions they take. Excellence is their goal, their target and even if they miss the mark, excellence shows up in their attitude and the way they deal with defeat. A person of Excellence not only believes in himself, but also believes in their team and the best that they can be. As you attract like-minded and like-hearted individuals to be on your team you must realize that you attract who you are. You as the leader, must portray the right internal components

The Customer Experience

and realize that the energy you send out is going to be mirrored in the candidates that show up to play on your team. Energy begets energy.

Consider what type of energy, attitude and vibration you're sending out. Are you the kind of person you would like to hire to be on your own team?

48   CHRISTOFFJWEIHMAN.COM

Chapter 4

EMPOWERMENT

"If we tell people what to do, we get workers.
If we trust them to do their jobs, we get leaders."

Simon Sinek

Education-Training

Now that you have your A-Team assembled, what's next?

I once heard an intriguing statement by Tony Robbins. He asked, "Are sales people made or born? They are found" he said. "Great sales people, great marketing people, are found and then they are trained to become better."

The same is true with great customer service people. So, you've found great customer service team members and yes, they are skilled, they have knowledge, and they have the internal components that resonate with your vision and mission, but they still need training. Many organizations today, have as one of their core principles 'Continuous Improvement' and this must include the category of Training. Many companies, especially in the hospitality industry have a very robust, in-depth, intense initial training program. They truly excel at onboarding their talent, but once they receive that initial training, they often never receive further training. It is not uncommon in the restaurant industry to hear a server or bartender say, "I've been doing this for 20 years." My question is, "How much additional training have you had in the past 20, 10, 5 years?"

When I spoke at the National Customer Service Association conference in Atlanta, I had a conversation with my bellman about customer service. I mentioned that I was speaking at the conference being held in the hotel where I was staying. He asked me if the principles of customer service change throughout the years. I told him that the basics certainly remain the same, however, there's always new thoughts and insights being put forth all the time. He didn't seem to hear the second part of what I was saying. He then pulled out his phone and he showed me a picture of a certificate of excellence award he received from attending a customer service training.

I complimented him on his achievement. But then I as I looked closer at the certificate I noticed the date on it; October 2002. It is admirable that he takes pride in his job and at one time he received an award for it. However, it saddened me to consider that this service professional had not had any additional training in 15 years. Wow! Fifteen years is a long time to be on a job and not receive any updated training. Even five years is a long time. Yes, I may be quite biased since this is the business that I am in, of inspiring and motivating people and companies to elevate their customer service.

Why should a company invest time and money into ongoing training? Providing regular and on-going training helps keep the morale of the team up. It communicates to them that you as a leader value them enough to invest in them. It communicates that you have certain standards that you expect them to uphold. A company that trains their people will stay on the cutting edge of technology and industry insights and best practices.

The 4 Pillars of Customer Service Excellence

I.   Internal Components (Soft skills, intangibles)

In the previous chapter we discussed these.

1.   Mindset, Attitude and Positive Energy
2.   Passion
3.   Servant Heart
4.   Personal Pride
5.   Commitment to Excellence

II. Skills, Techniques & Knowledge

This is the technical and mechanical aspects of one's job. As a waiter I must have the technical skill of how to open a bottle of wine, how to pour. I also need the knowledge of the different types of wine, what food they pair with, ability to detect the flavor nuances etc. I must have the skill of traymanship-properly carrying a tray of food or beverages. Each job in every industry has their own set of skills, techniques and knowledge. This is the area that most often is focused upon in training. This pillar is very important but it is not more important than any of the others.

III. Customer-Centric Mentality

All the skills and knowledge in the world will not help an individual if they cannot master being customer focused. The needs of the customer must be paramount in the minds and the attitudes of all team members, from leadership on down.

Having a Customer-centric or customer-focused Mentality means that we view our actions and processes through the lens of how it will affect our customers. Is this new policy going to cause our customers to love us more or will it make them feel like we don't really care about them? Is what we are doing in the best interest of our customers (that includes our internal customers-our employees) or merely in the interest of cutting costs? A Customer-centric Mentality is a vital pillar in Customer Service Excellence. Like the other three, it is equally important as the others.

IV. Creating a Culture of WOW!

This final pillar is about making sure that our vision, our mission and our purpose is being acted out on a daily basis. Service excellence is not just something that happens periodically. Rather, our commitment to elevating the customer journey must permeate everything that we do. Everyone in the organization is marching to the same beat. We all are striving for excellence in the customer experience. It affects how we talk with our customers on the phone, as well as how we converse with our co-workers in the lunch room. Everything we do, at all times, radiates who we are and what we stand for.

All of these pillars are of equal importance. However, often times training is focused only on the skills, techniques and knowledge. These are important for one to be effective in their job, however the other 3 Pillars are vital as well. Training programs throughout the year should touch on each of these areas. This will ensure your team's true effectiveness in serving your customers in the best way possible.

Regular training will help prevent your team members from adopting bad habits or poor methods of practice. As I stated previously, the old adage 'Practice makes perfect' is often quoted but it's actually a misconception. Let's say for example that I am learning to play golf on my own. If I swing my club in a particular incorrect manner and I practice that over and over again, I will not eventually become perfect in my swing. In fact, if I do not make the proper required adjustments to my swing I will merely succeed in teaching my mind and my body how to incorrectly perform that swing. I will create muscle memory and I will be very good at doing that thing in a wrong way.

Proper instruction, training and practice are necessary to become adept, efficient and proficient in anything. Whether I'm learning a new language, or how to give great presentations, or how to sell effectively, any new skill requires practice and proper instruction.

Customer Service is both a skill and an art. A skill can be learned. Art requires passion.

Training is vital to the growth of any organization because without it the staff often becomes stagnant and unmotivated. Training brings new life and energy to the team, especially if someone outside the company is brought in. It will invigorate and inspire the team. Providing training for your team equips them to perform more effectively, which in turn will directly affect the way your customers feel about their experience with your company.

Like Shep Hyken is fond of saying, "Training is not something you *did*. It is something you *do*. And you must do it often. Frequent and ongoing training is vital."

It is usually quite easy to identify companies that have periodic and ongoing training and those that have none or no further training beyond the initial onboarding. Those that do have team members that are more engaged. They tend to take more initiative. They know that they are being assessed on their performance and they are committed to the success of the company and themselves personally.

When an owner or manager invests in training for his team, this communicates a powerful message to all the members of that team. First, it conveys that certain standards are set and are to be met. Next, it says that he cares about the team enough to provide the tools and training necessary to be effective in their jobs. If that owner or manager is willing to put their money into providing training, it tells me that person is serious about the quality of service they provide for their customers.

Whenever I speak in front of a room of service professionals I always state my intentions:

1. **To Inspire**-the audience to imagine what is possible in terms of Service Excellence
2. **To Challenge**-them in their way of thinking. For only when one is open minded and willing to let go of some past ideas that are no longer serving us, can one receive new ideas.
3. **To Equip**-them with tools, techniques and strategies they can immediately implement to elevate the quality of service they provide and the quality of the experience their customers have.
4. **To Motivate**-them to take action now. Today. Sitting in training and listening, and even taking notes, is just a waste of time unless one is committed to taking action and making some change based upon what one just heard and learned.

There are many different types of training, but whether it be skill focused, technical, knowledge-based or personal development, I believe the above 4 intentions are vital to the success of any training program.

I challenge you to commit today to be a leader who consistently provides his team with proper, up to date, engaging, ongoing training. When you hire a trainer, whether it's someone from your corporate office or an independent, make sure that they are inspiring and not merely conveying technical information. Many employees dread going to training because it can often be uninteresting and uninspired. Learning can be fun and should be fun. Learning should be interactive and presented in a manner that is memorable, simple and fun. If you want your Team to feel, know and act empowered, you must provide the tools they need, and proper training is a necessary part of that.

How often do you provide training for your Team?

How much of your budget goes to training each year in comparison to how much you allocate for marketing & advertising?

What can you do now to provide more training for your Team?

What specific areas does your Team need more input on today?

Chapter 5

EMPOWERMENT-CONTINUED

As important as training is, all the training in the world can in one moment be rendered useless, null and void, if your team members do not feel empowered.

Employee empowerment is the next key component to exceptional customer experience.

Five Main Elements to Employee Empowerment

1. Trust
2. Communication
3. Authority
4. Responsibility
5. Accountability

Trust

Trust is vitally important to your Team being empowered and it must go both ways. You must trust your team to do their job well, and properly, without constant supervision. Likewise, your Team must trust you as their leader. In *Getting to WOW!* I talk about TMA (too much attention) versus TLA (too little attention) in regards to our customers. A guest wants to know that the server is available when they need something. On the other hand, they also do not want to feel like they are being gawked at during the course of their dining experience. The same principle applies with our team members. To put it simply and easy to remember:

No Ninjas and No Vultures.

Don't be a Ninja

A ninja moves about stealthily, too quickly to even make eye contact with, they appear and then disappear before one can respond or react. They make themselves invisible and unavailable. They hide in the shadows. These are great traits for a ninja, but terrible attributes for a manager or leader.

All team members want to know that their leader is available to them when they have questions or need help in making a decision. They want to know that the leader is there and that they have easy access to them. They must feel and know that they can trust and depend upon their leader for guidance and support.

I remember one manager at a restaurant that we frequent who actually would walk by the tables in the dining room with his hand shielding his face. He was present physically, but it was very clear that he did not want to deal with any problems. His Team was not able to depend upon him. This does not help build trust.

Don't be a Vulture

A vulture is constantly hovering, ready to pounce on it's prey. They never let their target out of their sight. They do not hide in the shadows. Rather they are always visible, circling from above or perched up high ready to attack

Again, great traits for a vulture, but not the kind of manager or leader one should aspire to be. You team must feel that you trust them to do their job with minimal supervision. Your Team members must know that you believe in them and that you are confident in their ability to do their job properly and well. Be available but don't be a vulture. Allow them to breathe.

Communication

Entire books have been written devoted to this subject alone. Therefore, I will not attempt here to rewrite or cover the entire topic. However, I would like to stress some very important key points.

First, communication as mentioned before, must be clear. There's a saying that "Clarity is power". That is true. When an employee is unclear on the communication it leads to confusion, and second guessing. Be clear when communicating with your Team. Yes, it seems simple, but like common sense, it is not always that common.

Communication must be a two-way street between you and your team members. An important part of your team being empowered is for them to feel the freedom to come to you as their leader and share their thoughts, problems, challenges and yes, even their feelings, with you as pertains to them performing their job. Nothing is more frustrating than for a team member being given an order and then the leader walking away without giving opportunity for questions to be answered or for clarification to be made.

The better and clearer you are in your communication to your team, the better example you set for them to follow.

Communication must be consistent. Do not presume that because you have stated something once-a policy, a procedure, an expectation, that everyone got the memo, and that it is in the forefront of their mind. We must remember that people do forget and often need to be reminded a number of times before something becomes second nature to them.

Communication must be open and honest. Again, the tone you set as a leader is the example that your team will follow. If you are open and honest, your team will know that you expect the same from them. Honesty is a great empowerer. Know the truth and the truth will set you free.

Communication must be respectful. Belittling, berating and other type of negative communication will lead to no positive outcome. Instead, be of a clear mind, devoid of heightened negative emotion when communicating with your team.

Authority

Your team members must know that they have the authority to do the job assigned to them. They must know that if delegated a task that they have been entrusted by leadership to perform that job. They must have the authority to make decisions as required for that task. Oftentimes, team members are expected or delegated to perform a task but they are not given the authority to do so. For example, in the tv show The Office, Michael the regional manager did not want to be responsible for choosing the healthcare plan for the team. So, to avoid having to make this unpopular decision, he delegated the task to Dwight. However, when Dwight set about to interview the employees to ascertain what would be the best healthcare plan, no one cooperated with him because everyone knew that Dwight didn't actually have the authority to make that decision.

If a team member is given a task, a role, a project to create, they must be given the authority to accomplish it. If it involves other departments or other team members, they too, must be informed that that person has been deputized, so to speak, to perform the task or make decisions pertaining to it.

Responsibility

A huge part of empowering your team is assigning responsibilities. There must be a clarity when it comes to each person's duties and roles. If one does not know what their true function is then they will constantly be guessing. This often happens in small and young companies. I am a fan of the show The Profit, starring Marcus Limonis. He helps struggling businesses become organized, focused and grow.

Quite often on the show when Marcus asks the key employees what their function is there is great confusion. "I am in charge of production and design, and sales", says one. The next person says, "Well, actually, I do most of the designing." One of the first things that Marcus establishes early on, is clearly defining the roles of each team member. For if one doesn't know what they're meant to be doing, they will not feel empowered, they won't expect to held accountable and they won't know what they have authority to do. It's simple but it's importance cannot be overstated. Define all roles.

Accountability

Patrick Lencioni puts it very directly in his excellent book on organizational leadership entitled, *The Advantage.* In it he states, "To hold someone accountable is to care about them enough to risk having them blame you for pointing out their deficiencies."

I would say that is a very good partial definition of accountability. I resonate with the idea that holding one accountable actually means that you care for them. You care about them living up to their promise, their commitment and potential.

Accountability is not always only about pointing out another's deficiencies. Rather, it is a tool to help your team be the best that they can be. Without accountability, there is no team cohesion, there is no glue that binds the group together. We all are playing on the same team. Therefore, when one of us hits or misses a shot, it affects us all. We win or lose together.

In *The Advantage*, Lencioni also talks about the importance of "creating a cadence of accountability". Accountability should be a regular, not a sometime thing. There should be a rhythm established by the leadership, with frequent meetings where team members are held accountable for results. All team members must know what is expected of them.

Holding your team accountable is a sign of a strong leader. It requires that you follow through with your commitment, your promise to lead your team to greatness. They will only get there with you leading the charge and holding them to account. This does not mean being a strict-by-the-book-only-no-mercy-or-understanding-ever, type of leader. Of course, there are exceptions to rules. But it is about setting a standard. More on this in chapter 11 on Excellence.

Coach AND Cheerleader

To empower your team is to help them reach their potential. In order to empower your team, you must be both their coach and their cheerleader. The word coach, according to Kevin Hall in his book, *Aspire*, "originated from a village in Hungary, called Kocs. This village is where skilled wheelwrights crafted the world's most beautiful and finest horse-drawn vehicles. These vehicles borrowed their name from the small township where they were skillfully designed and came to be known as 'coaches'."

"A coach is something or someone, who carries a valued person from where they are to where they want to be."

You as your team's leader, are their coach, regardless of whether that is your title or not. That is part of what you do. You help them reach their goals. You help carry them from where they are to where they desire to be. This is empowerment.

You also, are their cheerleader. You lift their spirits, you raise their morale, you set the bar for the positive attitude and energy as they take the field, step on the stage, walk into their place of work. With you cheering them on, they know that they are well equipped for the task at hand, you trust them and they know they will be successful.

You give them credit when they bring you inspired ideas. You acknowledge and applaud them as they assume the responsibility, however great or small you have given them. With an empowered and inspired team, you are on the road to success and your customers will greatly benefit as well.

Chapter 6

ENLISTMENT

"Loyalty is a cohesive force that forges individuals into a team"

John Wooden

H ere's a simple question that you must know the answer to as a leader; Are your team members on board? Have you enlisted them to buy in? Your team members must feel ownership of the organization's mission, the goals and the grand vision. It may not have originated from or been initiated by them-that's a given. However, they must in attitude, action, and speech, convey that they indeed are in alignment with them.

Loyalty and Allegiance

One test of whether you are truly a strong leader is if your people follow through on what you expect them to do the same when you are absent as when you are present. Do they have the same standards for their work on the days you are off, as when you are working? Do they slack off just a bit when you're not around? Are you constantly having to clean up messes and put out smoldering fires when you return from vacation? Perhaps this has more to do with company culture than just your leadership. Does their loyalty only last while you're physically present?

"I'm more concerned with who you are behind my back than who you are in front of my face. Your loyalty shouldn't depend upon my presence" Unknown

Allegiance and loyalty is something very personal. There will always be some people on your team or in your organization who probably don't belong, are not a good fit, and who don't resonate with the mission that you've laid out. It is important to not assume that just because someone shows up for work that they are on board and in sync with what you are attempting to accomplish. Why is this important to the overall customer experience? Because without this commitment you are left with walking zombies-who are going through the motions but who have no heart for what they're doing. They're here merely for a paycheck or until something better comes along.

These are the ones who are not concerned with the customer's emotional journey because they are not (in)vested in anything more than doing their job and getting paid for it. They themselves may not be experiencing a positive emotional journey. Don't assume they're on board. Ask them. This goes for any type of organization; a company, a non-profit, a sports team or otherwise. Some of your team may be showing up for practice, but they are not putting their heart into it. They lack something. Commitment, drive, vision.

How do we get our team to buy in?

Incentives are good but they are only external. They are good motivators but what happens when the incentives go away? There must be a driver that springs from within the individual. That is why I am always stressing the importance of passion. If one does not enjoy what they do, if they do not gain some internal satisfaction from doing their job well, then they will not be onboard. But even those who are passionate about what they do, want to be acknowledged, recognized, and asked by their leaders to be committed.

The Office

One of my favorite tv shows is The Office, starring Steve Carrell as Michael the District Manager of Dunder Mifflin Paper Company, and Rainn Wilson as Dwight K. Shrute, Assistant to the District Manager. Michael had some good leadership traits, however, he also was very flawed. One thing that always shown through with Michael was his authenticity. Many times, he was unknowingly, overbearing and insensitive, and often, he had no filter when he spoke. I believe it was his likeability and his realness that caused the staff to stick with him year after year. He was not the smartest, nor even the most charismatic leader, but he was real. And he asked his team to stand by him and to give him their commitment. He understood very well the principle of Enlistment. Authenticity in a leader is often the glue that keeps the team loyal.

Everybody's Favorite Radio Station is WIIFM

A group of individuals who are committed to a cause, a mission, a vision, something greater than themselves, will willingly give of themselves, their time, effort, energy, even their own resources if they believe that ultimately there is something in it for them.

WIIFM is everyone's favorite radio station. **What's In It For Me**?

As leaders, it is smart for us to tune in to that station-**WIIFM** often and hear our team when they ask, "What's in it for me?" Better yet, let's preempt their question by stating clearly our purpose, our vision, our overall goal and how it will be to *their benefit* as well.

Follow the example of Politicians-just this once

This happens all the time when a politician is running for office. Isn't it remarkable how they can get hundreds or even thousands of people to happily volunteer their time and energy for weeks, months or years to help them get elected to office? Yes, it may seem that these volunteers are doing it out of the goodness of their heart. But the truth is, they're doing it, sacrificing, because they believe their candidate will accomplish something that will benefit them. Their campaign speeches and slogans are full of promises of how they're going to make things better for those that help them get elected.

INSPIRE BELIEF

Oftentimes, it comes down to belief. People will give their allegiance if they truly believe that what that individual they are supporting or following, stands for, their vision, their mission, is going to help them. But those politicians do not assume. They are constantly asking their team of volunteers, "Do you believe? Are you committed? Do you see the vision, and can I count on you? And do I have your vote?"

Whatever type of organization you are leading, it would be to your advantage to periodically ask your team, "Are you committed, and can I count on you?"

A *Volunteer* Military

The same holds true in the military-at least in the United States, people volunteer to serve. I don't mean to oversimplify it because each person enlists for different reasons. However, a part of that reason for many, the driving force, is something outside of themselves. They believe they are contributing to a greater good-a common vision.

People will enlist when they feel that their service and participation is adding value to a higher purpose.

I recently read a great book entitled, *Sacred Commerce*, by Matthew and Terces Engelhart. In it they speak of "The Power of Making Requests".

They explain that when we make requests of our team we are "inviting them to participate" and an invitation trumps a requirement every time.

Consider the following words and the feeling you have when you hear them:

Demand, Requirement, Mandatory, Compulsory, Obligation, Edict, Command, Direction, Compel

What comes to mind, what emotion do you feel when you consider those words? The above words do not convey the idea of choice and they don't have a strong positive resonance.

Now consider the following:

Request, Invitation, Ask, Appeal, Seek

What emotion, what energy do you feel when you think of these words? The above words convey a feeling of willingness that comes from the individual because they've been *asked* to do something, rather than *commanded*.

There is certainly a different feeling and energy between the two sets of words and their implied meaning. I am not suggesting that we plead or beg our team. We simply need to request.

We must also continue to paint the picture of the greater mission and let each member understand and realize that they are an integral part to the overall success of the whole.

I recall a story that Michelle, my wife, told of how one day she invited the hospital housekeeper to join the nurse's morning huddle. Why? Because Michelle not only wanted her nursing Team to know who the housekeeper was, put a face to the role; she also wanted to stress the importance and value that even the lowest paid person on the Team contributes to the overall success of the organization. For if the housekeeper does not do her job well, of cleaning and sterilizing the rooms after each patient is discharged, then the nurses cannot do their job well. The next patient coming into that room could be in serious jeopardy of becoming sicker.

Michelle not only introduced Brenda, the housekeeper, she acknowledged and praised her in front of the team.

In order for your team members to buy in, they must believe that what they personally do in the company matters, and that it contributes to something greater.

> *By each of us doing our job well, with a positive attitude, and with a smile in our hearts, we each contribute to the overall success of the organization.*

Each team member must know that they have value and that they are more than a number, a body filling a position, more than a cog in the wheel.

No one ever is irreplaceable, the story of Steve Jobs getting fired from the company he founded is a great reminder of that. However, everyone should feel that they bring value to the team.

Those that are not inspired to fully enlist themselves in the organization's mission, purpose and goal will ultimately self-select themselves to be let go or will decide to move on.

If we desire commitment from our team we must show them the future, paint the picture and help them see how they are a part of the vision. We must inspire belief, and give the call to action and put forth our request and ask them, "Are you on board?" And if they are, then it is much easier for you to lead your team to set sail towards your organization's goal of Customer Experience Excellence.

Chapter 7

ENVIRONMENT

"The environment is everything that isn't me"
Albert Einstein

Think of a time when you went to a place of business, any business. It could be a restaurant, a spa, your drycleaners, a law office, a daycare, any type of business. What did you see when you walked in? What colors were prominent? What did you smell? Was there a distinct aroma in the air? Was it pleasant? How did it make you feel? What did you hear? Was it a place that was calm and peaceful? Or was it noisy and chaotic? Did the noise level make it easy to communicate with the staff or did you have to raise your voice to be heard?

Although the main focus of *The Customer Experience* is about the interaction and personal connection between you and your customers, I felt I would be remiss to not address the topic of environment. Many factors contribute to the overall environment or atmosphere and these together, or separately, can positively or negatively affect a customer's experience. Environment sets the mood and the tone and can have a subtle or dramatic influence on your customer before the two of you ever meet. Consciously and unconsciously, environment plays a very powerful role in the customer experience.

It's important for you to control what you can, then work with what you got, as there will always be some factors that we absolutely can do nothing about except to acknowledge the situation and move on.

Beyond Your Control

Location-Yes, location is super important and communicates a great deal about your business and does often strongly influence a customer's first impression-their perception of the business. Let's assume at this moment though, that your location is set, you're locked into a lease and there's nothing you can do about it currently. There's nothing you can do to change the actual geographic location of the business. But there's lots you can do to improve the perception a customer might have, especially if your business is in a less than desirable part of town. You can most certainly clean up the parking lot and rid the area of any eye sores-trash or debris in the front or immediate surroundings of the business. Control what you can, deal with what you've got and move on.

Color

It is no secret that color affects a person's mood, can influence their feelings, and can even compel them to take action. Color is powerful. Advertising agencies, marketing professionals and fast food restaurant chains have known this for at least fifty years. Have you ever wondered why nearly all fast food chain restaurants have some combination of red, yellow and white in their décor, logo and motif? Aside from their signs being very eye grabbing from the highway, those colors in combination, cause people to feel or believe that they are hungry. Whether you like their food or not, we have to acknowledge that McDonalds must be doing something right, having served billions of people worldwide.

How might we be able to utilize color to have a positive impact upon our customer's experience? Just like the location, you may not be able right now to change the color of the interior or exterior of your building. You may not be able to repaint the walls of every office in your company but there are some things that you can affect personally.

What are You Wearing?

Consider your attire-your wardrobe. What colors do you tend to wear? Do you wear colors that evoke warmth and kindness, brightness and cheerfulness? Or do you wear colors that convey an energy of coldness and indifference? Of course, some people work in roles in which they are required to wear a specific uniform. But inasmuch as you are afforded some flexibility, I encourage you to be cognizant of the colors you wear and the effect it may have upon your customers.

For example, if you work in an Italian restaurant or bistro, it is very common that the staff wear black shirt and black pants. Why? Black is considered formal and elegant. However, even if you are required to wear black shirt and black pants, perhaps you can determine the color of tie you wear. Even something as seemingly insignificant as this can have a powerful subconscious impact upon your customer's mood.

My wife, Michelle, as I've mentioned, is an ICU Supervisor in a major hospital. Hospitals are *not* necessarily known for exuding cheerfulness and positive energy. Let's face it, the majority of the people who are there-the customers/patients are sick. They're not typically in good positive moods. They are probably experiencing a low vibrational energy, and aren't feeling great.

The medical team, the doctors, the nurses, every single staff person, has the opportunity to bring positivity, joy and cheerfulness to these customers. Michelle is not only a normally very positive, upbeat and cheerful person, she also consciously uses color to bring even more brightness and cheer to the ICU. What do I mean, specifically? Yes, it is true that all medical staff are required to wear scrubs, but today scrubs come in every color and pattern and motif imaginable.

Michelle almost always wears bright colored scrubs with fun, whimsical patterns of puppies, or clouds or some kind of image that evokes joy, happiness and positivity. In addition to her scrubs, she is well known around the hospital by patients and staff alike, for her bright pink clogs. Many times, patients have commented to her about her pink clogs. They can see her coming from afar down the hallway. Michelle makes a conscious decision in choosing her attire. Sure, she does it because wearing a colorful wardrobe makes *her* feel good. But she also does it because she knows that it can *help make her patients and her team feel good.* She is very aware that something so simple can positively affect her patients.

There are so many ways that you can consciously utilize color to invoke or create a positive emotion or response in your customers.

Conversely, one could negatively affect a person's mood by wearing colors that look drab and dreary. If you are in sales, wearing gaudy colors may not be a great idea. What you are wearing may be so distracting that a customer is unable to focus on what you are saying because your shirt or outfit is WAY TOO LOUD!!

One other way that Michelle utilizes color is with her choice of hair color. Her hair is naturally reddish brown but since I've known her it's been many colors, red, black, pink, purple. She tells me that when she has shades of pink or purple highlights in her hair, that patients respond to her more positively. It conveys an approachability that maybe otherwise patients may not feel.

1. What colors are you consciously using in your personal attire and wardrobe? What affect are they having on your customers?
2. Are there any colors that you are using/wearing that may be having a subconsciously detrimental affect upon your business?
3. What about your marketing materials, your website? When people look at them how do they feel?
4. How would you want them to feel?
5. What might you change in your use of color in your business?

Lighting

Have you ever felt like you were in the dark? I mean literally, in the dark. Perhaps it was at a highly recommended, romantic restaurant, where once you were seated it was so dimly lit that the one tiny candle on the table was barely enough to see your partner's face. Candlelight can be very romantic, however, it should not cause one to strain to see what is right in front of him.

The type, color and intensity of lighting in any business can have a profound affect upon both the employees as well as the customers. As an owner, or business leader you should be keenly aware of what effect lighting is having on your business.

Studies have shown that fluorescent lighting in the workplace can cause anxiety, headaches and low productivity in employees. Poor lighting has also been shown to contribute to low employee morale and even disharmony amongst co-workers.

Natural sunlight is best for productivity. While indirect, recessed lighting has been found to be effective in creating a better atmosphere for workplace proficiency and harmony.

Perhaps it's something that has never crossed your mind. But giving attention to the lighting in your business could be the difference between frustrated customers and happy customers. It can make the difference between highly productive, cheerful staff and a lethargic and apathetic team. A space need not be nearly dark save for a single candle on the table to be considered romantic. It is not romantic if it causes frustration for the average customer to read the menu or to decipher what is on the plate set before him.

Creatively choosing a color palette that contributes to a romantic setting such as black and red, or purple, can be more effective than just merely dimming the lights as low as possible.

Now contrast that with the effect of lighting at a church service. The Church we attend in Las Vegas is called The Crossing. Every year they end their Christmas service in the exact same way. First, they completely dim the lights, in this situation it is appropriate because there is nothing that anyone needs to see or read.

Next, they begin lighting the candle of the person at the end of each aisle and then that person does the same to the person next to them and so on and so on. Before the candles are lit, the almost complete darkness is appropriate to the situation and the customer experience (yes, churchgoers are customers). In this situation the darkness creates feeling of positive anticipation, stillness, reverence and worship.

Once the candles are lit and the entire sanctuary is aglow from a thousand lit candles, this now creates a feeling of oneness and community, as together, we all sing Silent Night. Singing the song Silent Night together with the congregation certainly can bring a feeling of joy and peace to anyone. However, the use of lighting in the manner just described completely elevates the customer/worshipper's experience.

> *Lighting in your place of business should be congruent with the type of feeling and atmosphere you are desiring to create. Be mindful, be conscious and be creative.*

A multitude of moods and feelings can be created merely with the strategic use of lighting. A spotlight on the stage can make a performer feel like a star. A dimly lit parking lot can make someone walking to their car feel fear of someone lurking in the shadows. Dimming the lights on a competition show like American Idol, or Dancing with the Stars, creates a mood of suspense and anticipation for the contestants and the viewers. Lighting at a funeral can create reverence and respect and even sadness. While too much light in some instances may make a person self-conscious.

How can you use lighting to enhance your customer's experience?

Could changing the lighting in your business improve the mood or productivity of your employees?

How might you creatively use lighting to have a more positive effect upon your customers?

Sound/Noise/Music

> *"A noisy arcade is a good thing; a noisy dentist's office is not."*

Just as color and lighting are very effective in creating the desired mood for your place of business, so too, sound can also be used strategically. A coffeeshop where patrons come to study, do work, and even have business meetings ought to have a different ambience and type of music than a bustling restaurant or shopping mall. A small trickling counter-top waterfall can create a mood of relaxation in a spa, salon or dental office. However, one would not expect to see one in a children's recreation center or at a crossfit gym.

Consider what are the feelings that your customers feel when they come into your place of business and what are the feelings or mood you want to create for them.

I recall a time when Michelle and I went to a casual, healthy, organic eatery in Las Vegas. The place is well lit, bright and welcoming. The food is organic and delicious. The staff are cheerful and friendly. The music playing, however was not ambient, background and in fact it was heavy metal. I'm not criticizing heavy metal, if you enjoy it, great. However, it just didn't fit the mood and atmosphere this restaurant was attempting to create. Hearing that music blasting in the background was very irritating and unsettling for me and did not make for a pleasant dining experience. It bothered me so much that I went to the counter and asked a team member if they could possibly change the station or the genre of music. The answer? "No, we have to play whatever corporate sends to us. We have no way of adjusting it."

Contrast that with a gym experience-where I am taking Crossfit training. I still do not enjoy heavy metal music, but it is appropriate for that environment and the desired mood that the trainer is wanting to create-high energy, fast pace, heart pounding, excitement. It completely works for that environment and the desired end result.

Hopefully, you work in a business where you can control what type of music is being played. Consider the atmosphere you're wanting to create and make sure the style and genre of music is *contributing to* rather than *in conflict with* that mood. Also, be aware of the volume. The type of music being played may be appropriate for the business, but the sound level may be too high and that causes distortion and irritation for your customers.

Every business is different and will have different needs in terms of the sound atmosphere they're attempting to create. If your business needs a lively, upbeat mood then your sound/music choice will differ from a business that is creating a calm and relaxing environment.

One national company that I feel is not aware of the noise factor is a large retail store that has a red circle with a red dot in the center as their logo. All the team members, regardless of role, or department they are in, carry walkie talkies which are always turned up very high. It never fails that when I'm browsing in the aisles I always hear the squawk of the walkie talkies and team members talking back and forth with each other.

Squawk, "Does any team member know if we still have Christmas ornaments?"

Squawk, "I think those were moved to aisle 37 after the remodel."

Squawk, "Hey, Kevin, can you cover me, I'm 30 minutes late for going on break."

Squawk, "I'm with a customer right now, as soon as I get finished here, I'll relieve you."

Do I expect a retail store to be absolutely quiet and peaceful? No. But do I believe I should be subjected to this constant squawking and talking between team members which has absolutely nothing to do with me? No way!

Be conscious and aware of the noise in your place of business and consider whether it's appropriate and if it contributes to the overall customer experience or not.

AROMA

What's that smell? That could be a good question or not. It could mean 'what's that lovely fragrance?' Or it could mean, 'What is so stinky?'

One aspect of environment that may be easily overlooked by business owners is aroma. The power of scent and certain aromas is linked to our memories. Imagine your favorite aroma, maybe it's fresh baked cookies and it brings you back to your childhood and fond memories of your grandmother. Perhaps you love the scent of vanilla, cinnamon, or the smell of new car leather. There's no question that aroma can have a powerful affect upon us.

Some hospitals, spas and wellness centers diffuse essential oils to stimulate a feeling of relaxation, well-being and tranquility. There are many companies that make essential oils. Personally, I am a huge fan and user of DoTerra oils.

Some businesses have aromas that are unintentional but they would do well to pay better attention to and to take care of them. More than a few times, I have walked into a restaurant or bar and as soon as I set foot inside the door, I am hit with the overwhelming stench of stale urine. The problem is not necessarily that they don't clean their bathrooms often enough-although sometimes it's simply that. Rather, many times it's a situation where the entire building needs a deep cleaning below the surface. I'm not an expert in this, I just know that such an experience is so uninviting that I do not stay and give my business to such a place. In such instances, I will usually inform the manager. The sad fact is that I had to tell them. It is not easy running a restaurant or any business, but if the front of the restaurant smells of urine, it may cause one to question the overall hygiene or sanitation of the rest of the place.

Some businesses, like most of the Hotel Casinos on the Las Vegas Strip are not only very conscious when it comes to the aromas in their place of business, they are actually very intentional about it. Nearly every Las Vegas Strip resort vaporizes highly aromatic oils into their duct system where the airflow dilutes and distributes them throughout the inside of the entire property.

If you've ever been to Las Vegas and walked into any hotel on Las Vegas Blvd. you'll know exactly what I'm talking about. Each hotel has a very distinct aroma. Some are stronger than others, while others, are more subtle. Most of these hotels use a system developed by Mark Peltier, President of a company called AromaSys.

He has created signature aromas, and unique to, each hotel. The Mirage's scent is Polynesian, Mandalay Bay's aroma is Southeast Asian, and the Bellagio has the scent of Northern Italy.

You may decide to go the route of the Las Vegas casinos and use a company like AromaSys to develop scents that are unique to your business and locations. Or you could choose to diffuse some DoTerra oil blends in your business. Doing so, could help create the mood and atmosphere that is inviting and welcoming to your clientele. Do not underestimate the power and potential positive effect aroma can have on your customers.

CLEANLINESS

Perhaps this is a topic that should not have to be mentioned. However, the cleanliness of your place of business or lack thereof can and does have a powerful affect upon your customers. If the reception area is not well organized, with magazines strewn all over the tables, trash overflowing, dust on the shelves-these things are all a reflection of you, your company and how you feel about your customers. Your reception area is your physical statement of welcome to your clientele. Take a moment and walk into your place of business and view the area with the eyes of one who's never been there before. Walk up to the check in counter, sit in a chair that a guest would sit in. Scan the room, is it tidy and well kept? Are the seats clean and comfortable? How about the other furniture-the coffee tables, are they smudged and dirty?

Restrooms

The cleanliness and hygiene of a restroom at a restroom or any place of business is a strong indicator or what the rest of the place is like. If the restroom is untidy, dirty, not clean, then I would place a strong bet that the kitchen is also not clean. I have often gone to a restaurant and first walked into the restroom, if it was not up to par, then I chose not to eat at said restaurant.

You may say, well, you're in retail or you're in real estate or some other industry where you're not preparing food. Why does it matter about the cleanliness of the restroom? It matters because every part of the business, yes, even the restroom is a reflection and a statement about you and your business. Also, the restroom is for your customers, it speaks of how you value them. If you tell me you value your customers but your place of business is not tidy, clean and well kept, then I would say there is a disconnect.

Simple things go a long way in communicating a welcoming first impression to your prospects and clients.

PHYSICAL COMFORT

Many a time I've been to a restaurant or bar that had trendy, beautiful décor and furniture. They have these amazing, expensive looking barstools, but when I sit in them, I am thoroughly disappointed. They gave no comfort whatsoever. I often wonder if the owner simply purchased the furniture based upon how it looks and price, rather than on how it actually feels to sit in them. I am amazed at how many venues where I find this to be the case. My question is, did they order these furniture pieces without actually sitting in them? You have hundreds, perhaps thousands of customers that will be sitting in these chairs, barstools, sofas, etc. over the course of many years. Don't you want them to feel comfortable when they are dining or drinking in your place of business? How about the chairs or sofas in your reception area-are they comfortable to sit in? Have you ever sat in one yourself?

How about the chairs in your office? Are they positioned so far away from your desk that one has to almost shout to communicate with you? Imagine your prospect is seated across from you in your office. They are truly interested in the product or service that you are offering, but they cannot really pay attention to you because the chair they are sitting in is just so uncomfortable. Can a chair lose the sale for you? Potentially, yes.

We need to literally put ourselves in the place of our customers. Walk into your reception area with the eyes of your customer. Stand where they stand. Sit where they would be seated. Is that beautiful black leather sectional sunk so deep that when your customer sits down they have a difficult time standing up?

Consider who your clientele are-specifically their age. If you are a personal injury attorney or a business that caters to senior citizens, consider if the furniture is truly comfortable and appropriate for people who many have difficulty with mobility.

TEMPERATURE

The temperature of the environment also can have a positive or negative affect upon your employees' mood, attitude and productivity. Too cold-and they'll spend their time distracted and trying to stay warm. They will not be fully productive. Too warm and they may become lethargic and sleepy. Be cognizant of the temperature in your business and observe what affect it may be having on your clientele and your team.

By now, it should be very evident that environment can either work for us, or against us, in affecting the customer experience. If we are consciously aware and creative about it, our surroundings can be our silent positive partner enhancing the experience for every customer that walks into our place of business.

Chapter 8

EXPECTATIONS

"High expectations are the key to everything."

Sam Walton

One of my favorite books is *The Four Agreements* by Don Miguel Ruiz. It espouses a very simple and truly profound philosophy, a powerful code of conduct that can transform how we live our lives and experience freedom, true happiness, and love. One of those Four Agreements simply states, "Make no Assumptions". To me that is very similar to 'have no expectations', because an expectation is an assumption. I agree with that when it comes to my personal life and interaction with others. I do not, however, agree when it comes to business, working with teams and the customer experience.

It's quite easy to find many quotes that align with the 'No expectations' philosophy;

"No expectations, no disappointments";

"How to be happy-Don't expect a damn thing from anyone";

and

"The secret to happiness is-low expectations."

I get it when it comes to my life, to personal relationships etc. I somewhat agree. Oftentimes, we have unrealistic expectations of others, or of a situation we find ourselves in. Sometimes we place unreasonable expectations on our children, our spouses, people close to us. That is certainly not good. But that is not what we are speaking of here.

In the business world the above quoted statements simply will not cut it, especially when we are talking about customer service and the customer experience.

No, instead I will line up alongside the likes of Sam Walton and Sir Richard Branson.

Walton said, "High expectations are the key to everything." We'll expound upon that in a moment.

Sir Richard Branson stated, "The key is to set realistic customer expectations and then not to just meet them but to exceed them, preferably in an unexpected way."

The underlying meaning of the 'Have no expectations' philosophy is that if you have none, then you'll never be disappointed. That logic unfortunately falls apart in the business world. We absolutely must have expectations. For if we do not, granted, we may be assured to never be disappointed, but we will also never be able to track progress, make adjustments or improvements, or account for growth.

For what are sales forecasts, company goals, or personal goals, or budgets, proposals, even schedules, and the like, if not *EXPECTATIONS?!*

Yes, I do understand that plants naturally grow and have no thoughts or expectations of if they'll grow. But that type of thinking is a bit too esoteric for me when it comes to the business world. As you know, I do believe in energy, the law of attraction, the power of our minds and the like, but I don't think it's being un-spiritual to think about, talk about and yes, to have expectations.

What are we talking about, specifically in regards to expectations? Expectations of whom or what?

EXPECTATIONS OF OURSELVES AND OUR TEAM

While we are still in the preparation, pre-customer interaction phase of creating the emotional journey, let's focus on ourselves first as leaders. We must hold ourselves accountable first, know what we expect of ourselves. For if we don't begin with ourselves, we cannot with integrity, hold our team members to account. Next, we must have expectations of our team as a whole, certain guidelines and standards.

Your mission statement is your declaration of the expectations of yourselves and of your team.

This is you stating "This is what we believe. This is what we stand for. This is what we expect of ourselves and our employees/team members. This is how we interact with, engage and serve our clientele."

Your Mission Statement and your core values combined together, are the promise that you make to your prospects and customers.

Your promise that tells your prospects and customers what they can and ought to expect from you, your company, your team. Your promise tells them, "This is how we serve you."

Getting taken to the cleaners

I am quite particular about how I like my clothes to be dry-cleaned. Every place has a different process. I went to one a couple times, told them how I'd like my clothes done and they assured me that they could and would accommodate my requests. However, each time I went to pick up my shirts, they were bunched tightly together in such a way that it caused the shirts to wrinkle the ones beneath them. I would bring this to their attention and they would apologize and redo them for me. Other times my buttons would be crushed or broken from the pressing.

Finally, after about the 4th time, I had a conversation with the manager. When I questioned him about the lack of quality in their work, he agreed with me. He acknowledged that they've missed the mark multiple times. He even said that they weren't delivering on their own standards. He then said, "We suggest that you just go somewhere else." I was flabbergasted. They stated what their standard and quality was and admitted they've been missing the mark. But rather than committing again to meet my expectations they just said 'goodbye' to me.

SILENT EXPECTATIONS CAN BE DEADLY

Expectations must be stated, communicated and understood by all team members. Silent expectations are deadly to the life and health of an organization. A leader who holds certain expectations in silence and only communicates them to the team once someone has not fulfilled them is not setting their team up for success. It is unwise, unfair and unhealthy to have unspoken expectations.

Expectations need to be clear, unambiguous and clearly communicated. A leader who constantly says a team member, "should know what is expected of them" can only rightfully do so, if indeed those expectations have been clearly communicated and not just once or twice. Nor is it sufficient that the expectation or requirement is simply noted in fine print somewhere in an employee handbook.

The book, *The 4 Disciplines of Execution* by Chris McChesney, Sean Covey, and Jim Huling, stresses the absolute importance of leaders *overcommunicating* to their team their goals and expectations. Companies in which the employees exude the company culture and philosophy, are one's where the expectations are clearly and consistently conveyed to all team members on a regular basis. If an employee says they 'Didn't know' or they 'Thought that…' it is really incumbent upon leadership to ensure that they do know.

Once we're set on expectations of ourselves and our team it enables us as an organization to:

1. Ascertain and better understand the expectations of our clientele.
2. Better equip our team to anticipate, meet and ideally, exceed our clientele's expectations on a regular basis-or at least to strive to.
3. Deliver the experience that they (our customers) may not even have known they wanted. (WOW! them)

Having expectations of ourselves and our team members is not about perfection, rather, it is about setting a standard of excellence.

CUSTOMER EXPECATATIONS

Expectations are a combination of what I call Requires and Desires, or needs and wants. So, which is more important for us to give our clients, their needs or their wants?

Answer: Both!

At times it may be wiser to give the customer what they want first. By doing so, we show that we care about them and their desires and that we are listening. It's not about us. It's about them. Once we've engaged them in that way, they're more likely to drop their defenses and be ready to receive what they truly need.

The delineation between what a client needs and wants may not always be evident. In such cases, give them both at the same time.

What do customers need and want?

All customers want to:

Feel welcomed
Be acknowledged
Respected
Engaged
Appreciated
Provided a good service/product at a good value

There are many things that a customer wants or expects. My good friend Adam Toporek has a wonderful book entitled, *Be Your Customer's Hero*. In it he talks about 7 trigger points that negatively affect the customer experience.

The 7 Trigger Points are:

1. **Being Ignored**- No one wants to be ignored or feel like they're not being seen or heard. This clearly is not great customer service. The customer should always feel they are being paid attention to, and that they're being heard.

2. **Being Abandoned**-Have you ever been at a place of business, say an office supply store, one staff member begins your order and then all of sudden they walk away? You have no idea what happened. They don't say anything to you. You're just left there, waiting, and wondering. This is very frustrating and does not make for a great experience.

3. **Being Hassled**-The service professional questions you, doubts you, even argues with you about something. The customer may not always be right, but they should be treated fairly, and not be stressed when doing business with you.

4. **Being Faced with Incompetence**-When a customer pays for a service to be done, they expect that it will be done correctly and properly. Incompetence is often the result of lack of proper training provided to the team members.

5. **Being Shuffled**-This often happens with customer service over the phone. A customer calls for something and they are sent from one department to another. Each time they have to repeat their situation to the new person on the phone who is trying to assist them. Being shuffled makes the customer feel they're not being taken seriously and their time is being wasted and oftentimes it ends with no satisfactory resolution.

6. **Being Powerless**-"I'm sorry sir, that's our policy." "I'm sorry ma'am there's nothing we can do about that." These and other similar phrases are so often repeated to customers and it leaves the customer frustrated, stressed and powerless.

7. **Being Disrespected**-Regardless of the situation, even if it gets heated, it is never acceptable to be rude to a customer. Even if the customer is out of place in their speech or their tone, the service professional must always remain respectful, patient, courteous and professional.

Customers are people and they want the same thing that all people do-for their experience of doing business with us, with you, with me, to be a positive and pleasant one.

Customers always have expectations, both conscious ones and subconscious ones. Our job is to anticipate and be proactive. We do not want to merely meet their expectations but to exceed and then blow them away. Meeting expectations is good, but it's boring and predictable. Be creative. Embrace the goal of exceeding your customers' expectations. You can elevate their experience by going above and beyond in your attitude and actions.

Where do Customer Expectations Come From?

A customer's expectations are informed by a number of factors. Expectations of today's customers have increased greatly compared to in the past. They are more educated, knowledgeable and aware. They understand the marketplace, are well-read and most have given much thought to what they expect from their experience where they spend their money. A customer that has no expectations is very rare-if not, nonexistent.

Their expectations can be based upon research they've done, word of mouth that they've heard, reviews, past experience or future anticipation. Be very aware. Every customer that comes into your place of business or who engages you in some manner, has expectations of what doing business with you looks like.

SUBCONSCIOUS NEGATIVE EXPECTATIONS

Sometimes their unconscious expectations may actually be negative. A customer who is not mechanically inclined or not very knowledgeable about auto mechanics may go to an auto repair shop and presume that he will be misled, or unfairly taken advantage of. He may believe that he will be charged for a part or repair that is not truly necessary. This is clearly not a good expectation for a customer to have. This, of course is NOT the expectation we want to meet. In this situation, the service professional, instead, must counter that expectation by building rapport and trust.

Another example may be when a couple has dined at a restaurant and the experience was fraught with problems, so the manager invites them to return to 'give them another chance'. When that couple returns they most likely, will have some negative expectations, some apprehension. The service professional must from the outset, acknowledge that the previous experience was not great and ensure the customer that this time will be above and beyond. And then they must deliver!

How sad and how often it happens that a company is given a second chance with a previously dissatisfied customer and they don't take every opportunity to simply blow them away. You have a second chance-you've got to do more than just your normal. You must create an out of the ordinary, memorable experience. You have what it takes to do that but it takes a conscious effort and some creativity.

THE CUSTOMER IS *NOT* ALWAYS RIGHT, BUT...

No, I do not believe the customer is always right. Sometimes they may have unreasonable or unrealistic expectations. However, their perception is always king. Even if you believe they are expecting something that you cannot meet or fulfill, you still have the power to create an amazing, exceptional experience for them. A powerful, positive experience may cause them to forget about what their original unrealistic request was.

> *Our goal must be to anticipate their expectations, meet and exceed them and create memorable experiences for our customers. It's not about whether a customer is right or not. It's about how they are made to feel. Do they feel special, acknowledged, well taken care of?*

That is the question we must always be asking ourselves. And hopefully the answer is yes.

Once we know and can anticipate the expectations of our customers, we will then be better equipped to fully engage them, creating a positive customer experience for them all the time, every time.

Chapter 9

ENGAGEMENT

"Highly engaged employees make the customer experience. Disengaged employees break it."

Timothy Clark

"The more you engage with customers, the clearer things become and the easier it is to determine what you should be doing."

John Russell, President-Harley Davidson

O utside of the business world in common parlance, engagement is a commitment between two people to get married. People usually become engaged when they are in love with each other, care for that other person's well-being and desire to share life's joys, struggles and adventures together with that one person.

Engagement is always a two-way, conscious commitment. I'm engaged to you and you're engaged to me. In relation to the customer experience there are two types of engagement to consider; Employee Engagement and Customer Engagement. In our previous chapter on Expectations, we discussed how important it is for leaders to first have expectations for themselves before placing expectations on their team. Likewise, we cannot expect our employees to successfully engage our customers unless we, as leaders, are committed to fully engaging our team.

EMPLOYEE ENGAGEMENT

There are many definitions of employee engagement and they all tend to include some common aspects.

Employee engagement is the extent to which employees feel passionate about their jobs, are committed to the organization and put discretionary effort into their work. (Find and quote the source)

Gallup, the polling and research company, defines engaged employees as those "who are involved in, enthusiastic about and committed to their work and their workplace."

The above two definitions are very similar. The key elements in each are; being passionate, being enthusiastic and being committed.

In the most recent research done by Gallup, the findings are quite revealing:

32.6% of American workers are engaged

54% of American workers are disengaged

17% are actively disengaged-meaning they are going out of their way, consciously, to speak ill of, or undermine the company where they work.

It is a well-documented fact across the board, in all industries, that an engaged employee will excel more at their job than a co-worker who is disengaged. Why? Because engaged employees are passionate about their job. They are committed to their own success as well as the success of their colleagues and they are committed to the organization's goals and vision. They are all in. These are the employees who are the right fit for the team. They are the ones who feel and know they've been equipped, trained and empowered. They are the ones who actually said "Yes" when asked if they are onboard. And they continue to say "Yes" on a daily basis.

A well engaged employee will deliver the best customer service experience every time.

The responsibility for your team members to be engaged falls both upon your shoulders as the leader, as well as upon the individual employee.

Considering the above stated statistic that only 32% of Americans are engaged at their work, it is no surprise that the customer experience across the board needs some elevation.

It is critical for us as leaders to realize that our employees are our first customers. They are our internal customers.

In one of my favorite books on Customer Service, *Amaze Every Customer Every Time*, by my friend and mentor, Shep Hyken, he states, "In the final analysis, of course everything everyone in your organization does affects the external customer experience. We have to amaze our internal customers if want our external customers to be amazed."

It is not our responsibility as leaders to instill passion in our team members. That must come from within them. However, it is vital that we create an environment where each employee believes that they have value and that they are an integral part of the overall success of the organization and that their role contributes value. It is incumbent upon us, however, that we are not merely filling positions when we hire, but rather we are consciously attracting the right candidates/team members who possess the internal components that resonate with the organization's mission, vision and core values.

Another great book on this topic, which I highly recommend is *Three Signs of a Miserable Job*, by Patrick Lencioni. In it Lencioni talks about how all employees want to know that what they do matters, that their boss cares about them, and how to measure whether they're doing a good job. (my paraphrase).

I have worked in many jobs/held many positions in a variety of companies throughout my career before starting my own business, and I can say that in most of them I did not feel or experience much engagement from my bosses.

I've always been a dedicated, hard worker, and committed to my success and to the success of the company in which I work. However, after a while of not being engaged by management or one's boss, it's easy to not care as much. It's easy to become disengaged.

I remember more than once, when I worked for a company wherein I had a leadership role and I was consistently taking my work home with me. If I wasn't completing some type of reports, then I was simply mentally taking the job home with me. I experienced many sleepless nights thinking about issues in the company. You may have experienced the same. Often, I would wonder if the boss really put in the same amount of care and concern for the company as I did and I was merely an employee. I'm sure they did, but I just didn't feel like it seemed that way.

How do we create engagement in our organization so that it's a two-way interaction? Employee engagement should be a core of the company culture and not merely a set of actions at a specific time.

One person I know that is very adept at both *employee* and *customer* engagement is my wife, Michelle. As an ICU Supervisor she works the day shift from 6am to 6:30 pm and beyond. She starts her shift every day with a morning huddle. During this very short meeting she gathers all her nurses on that shift and truly engages them. She'll often share a heartwarming or inspiring story. Maybe she'll read an uplifting excerpt from a book to them. She'll share about what they're doing right and areas that they can improve on. She will talk about certain patients and challenges that are in store for the day. She'll give acknowledgement and accolades to a team member who was caught in the act of doing something extraordinary. Maybe they'll be rewarded with a free lunch. (These are called 'Gotcha's)

What is the result of her huddles? Her team is engaged. They feel acknowledged, recognized and listened to. I know this because I've heard it from their own lips, either they've told me, or I've overheard them at a company party telling Michelle how much they appreciate her and her leadership.

Team members want to know that they are more than just a nameless employee. When you engage your team members, both as a group and individually, with love and trust and care and empowerment-they in turn, will engage your customers in like manner.

Don't be an Un-Engaged Boss

I'm a fan of the tv show, Undercover Boss. If you're not familiar, let me explain. In this show a CEO, owner, or high-level executive of a well-known company goes undercover in their own organization. They usually pose as a new employee or a candidate hoping to be hired full time. They perform the duties of various roles in the company. There are often some humorous scenes in which the Undercover Boss displays their lack of skill in performing some of the most basic tasks. Their lack of skill is either because it's been so long since they've done said task, or because they got hired as an executive and they actually have never performed that task. This is really not that big of a surprise. What is most revealing, is when the other employees the Undercover Boss is working alongside, share their feelings about the company, and specifically their feelings towards leadership.

They will often talk about the lack of engagement with the frontline employees. At some point during each episode, the executive has an epiphany and comes to the realization of how out of touch they've been with their employees. They make amends with their team and commit to making changes and to empower their team more going forward.

There are many ways to engage your team members. Each leader must find a manner and routine that fits him and his leadership style. But be mindful that if your team is feeling disengaged, a good part of that responsibility lies with you.

What exactly do we mean when an employee says they feel disengaged? To each person it may mean something different. At the heart of the feeling of disengagement often times, is a lack of passion for what they do. Perhaps they are feeling like they are not acknowledged, their ideas and suggestions are being overlooked by management. Maybe they feel that their contribution is not appreciated or noticed. Maybe they've never been told "great job" by a supervisor.

Something as simple as having a team huddle, which I described earlier, can be a very powerful means of creating engagement.

Engagement is Not a Sometimes thing

The key is consistency. Daily huddles at the start of the shift makes team members feel like they know what's going on, at least in their department. Holding consistent huddles builds more rapport between management and staff. Your team will feel more inspired.

Restaurants that are most successful are usually ones that have a daily line-up (similar to a huddle). During the line-up management usually will discuss some aspect of service or test team members on menu ingredients, they will explain the daily special, they will talk about how many and who has made reservations for the evening.

The manager may share a simple insight or a story or principle to inspire their team. The ones who get it, do it well and they help get their team into a positive state of mind, and a positive attitude and energy pervades them.

I've seen some restaurants where one might think they were witnessing a college sports team exiting the locker room to take the field. There is a palpable energy amongst the team as they go out to engage and serve their clientele with excitement and enthusiasm.

When leaders engage their team, their team members will feel and act engaged. They will move with purpose and conviction. They will raise their head high and have more confidence, knowing that what they do matters. They will actively and consciously initiate engagement with their customers rather than waiting for the customer to first engage and just responding to them.

Mark Moraitakis of Chik-Fil-A says, they teach their team members to be the first to smile, the first to greet their customers. The first to engage. It's a simple thing, but it is so powerful and effective.

Employees or team members who are engaged become a great *face* of your business, representing your company's mission, vision and core values. They may even be mistaken as upper management, or even the owner, because they conduct themselves in such a manner as if it was their own company.

Engaged employees are dependable, trustworthy and full of great ideas.

Engaged employees know their value and don't hold back or do the bare minimum required of them.

Engaged employees shine and make you and your leadership team look good.

The Power of P.R.A.I.S.E

Here's a simple and effective tool to consider when engaging your team, remember to P.R.A.I.S.E. them.

P **Proclaim** the good publicly. When a team member has done something out of the ordinary, exceptional, etc., proclaim it to the person in front of the entire team. This will make that person feel good for being noticed for their accomplishment. It will also stimulate morale and spur others onto achieve greatness as well.

R **Reprimand** in private. All too often, we see a staff member being scolded and berated by a supervisor or manager in front of their peers. This is unacceptable and is not proper engagement Such action embarrasses the team member, makes them feel small and negatively affects the morale of the team. This is certainly not a new concept, but it is startling to see how many leaders have failed to master this simple principle. Worse even, is when the team member is reprimanded in front of a client. This does not build greater rapport between you and your customer. Instead it will create a wall and even mistrust between the two of you. Always remember, if it is a reprimand, it needs to take place out of view and earshot of other team members and customers.

A **Acknowledge** challenges and opportunities for growth. This is different than reprimanding- that is when correcting someone for something specific that they've done wrong, a mistake etc. Acknowledge the challenges and opportunities for growth means to take an honest assessment of a situation. Is a particular team member, perhaps in a role that is not best suited to their skillset? Make the appropriate adjustment. Are there areas as a team that you need to focus on more? Point those opportunities out so that everyone is clear on what needs to be done or what needs to be done differently or better.

I **Inspire** to meet the challenges. Don't merely give instructions or commands to your team, better yet, as we discussed in the chapter on Empowerment, give requests. When you give such requests, you show your team that you are on their side. You believe in their success. Inspire them. Let them know you believe they are capable, qualified and more than able to complete the task, accomplish the goal, create an amazing final product. Whatever it is that you are desiring and requiring them to do, let them know and hear and feel from you that it is possible and they are the ones who are best fit to do this thing.

S **Support** -Give your team what they need to accomplish this task. Perhaps they need some coaching, maybe they need certain supplies. Whatever is required to help them be successful in this project provide it for them. Don't just say, "You've got this" and then leave them hanging. Let them know you are available to them. Perhaps they have questions, perhaps they need advice. Maybe they just need to have a boost of their confidence. Give them the support they need and then watch them shine.

E **Encourage, Evaluate & Ensure Success** -Everyone wants to be encouraged when they're attempting something new to know they're on the right track. People want to be encouraged if they're doing the job well or if they are not, they want to be encouraged that you know they are capable to do it. You must evaluate their progress and make any adjustments that may be needed to ensure their success. Your team still needs to be led, that's why you're the leader. They can do what you ask of them, assign to them or expect of them, but they will be more successful if you P.R.A.I.S.E. them.

CUSTOMER ENGAGEMENT

Once you have fully engaged employees or team members, they will be better equipped to deliver the best service experience to your customers.

What do all customers want?

> *Just as a well engaged employee will deliver the best customer service experience to your customers, in the same manner, a well engaged customer will become your best evangelist.*

To engage our customers means to be focused on them and their needs in this moment.

To engage our customers means to be present to them, with them and for them.

To engage our customers means anticipating their needs and proactively fulfilling and exceeding those needs.

To engage our customers means I am thinking about what they may be feeling, and doing my best to make this experience, pleasant, positive and enjoyable for them.

To engage our customers means making them feel welcome, listened to, respected and cared for.

Touching Tables

In the restaurant industry there is a term called touching tables. This is when the manager walks the floor and greets the diners, checking in with them, making them feel welcome. Restaurants that are most successful, tend to be ones where the practice of touching tables is common place. Managers should not wait until there is a problem or complaint before approaching a table. This practice of active engagement with the guests builds rapport with them, and it reduces the incidence of negative reviews. The guest feels that the management team actually cares about them, are happy they are there and appreciate their business.

Unfortunately, the practice of touching tables is less common than one might expect. All too often a manager only makes their appearance on the dining room floor once, and only if, a complaint has been made. Or if a guest actually requests to speak with a manager. By that time, the guest already has a not great perception of the restaurant, the team and their experience. By touching tables, we can show that we actually care about the guest experience and that our role as leaders is not merely to 'put out fires'.

Every industry has a different term or expression for this-in the hospital, my wife and her leadership team does leadership rounds-their equivalent to touching tables. When Michelle enters a room, one of the first things she does as she introduces herself, by name as part of the leadership team, is to praise her nursing team to the patient. She says something like, "Good afternoon, my name is Michelle, I'm part of the leadership team, I'm just checking in on you and making sure my team is doing an excellent job of caring for you. I have the best nurses in the hospital."

This type of engagement sets the customer/patient at ease. It makes them feel and know that they have access to leadership, if they do have a concern or complaint. It is a proactive approach which can create relationship of trust between the service professional and the customer.

Be Like Dr. Stokes

We've all met people who are really great at customer engagement. These individuals are fluent, adept and skilled in putting the customer at ease and setting the tone for a positive experience. One person who comes to mind is my dentist, Dr. Joel Stokes. He is such a master at making people feel comfortable. His demeanor is very gentle and he exudes positivity. He speaks in a calm reassuring manner.

I have not been to many dentists in my life, so I don't know if this is the norm. I'm guessing it's not, but I don't know. What I do know is that many adults, myself included, stay away from visiting the dentist because of fear.

When I met Dr. Stokes, I am embarrassed to say, that I had not been to a dentist in years. Many, many years. When I sought him out, I was in so much pain. Pain that I had been ignoring for a couple of weeks. Finally, in spite of my fear, I set the appointment. I do not do well with any kind of pain. But I knew that a tooth infection could turn septic and I could be in danger of something much worse than tooth pain.

When I first went to see Dr. Stokes, he didn't sit me down in his dental chair. Instead, he took me to his office and we talked. He didn't make me feel ashamed or embarrassed for my years of dental neglect. Rather, he assured me that that is very common. He explained his process and then he told me that his goal is for me to spend the least amount of time necessary in his chair. He told me that he treats every one of his patients with the same care and concern as he would his own family.

He said he would not recommend any treatment or procedure that he wouldn't also perform on his own family. He introduced a document called a Trust Contract which explains that it's a voluntary agreement and relationship between him and his patients. He made me feel empowered as a patient, rather than being in the dark.

I was so impressed by Dr. Stokes and his process. He truly understands his patients and what they are going through. He does every thing in his power to walk them through what to expect and he turns what could be a very frightening experience into something that is peaceful and positive.

I'm not saying that I am ecstatic about having dental work done. However, I do know that Dr. Stokes helped me overcome my fear of going to the dentist, as long as it is him. Dr. Stokes, truly understands customer engagement and sets an example that we can all learn from regardless of the type of business we have.

The Property Brothers

Another person, actually two people, who are perfect executioners of great customer engagement, are Drew and Jonathon Scott, stars of the tv show Property Brothers. These two are a brother duo who buy and sell homes. They help families find houses that need renovation and they fix them up for them. These two guys are absolute masters at customer engagement.

Everyone who's ever bought or sold a home knows that it can be very stressful experience. It is often a rollercoaster ride of emotions. When a renovation is taking place there's often unexpected situations and unplanned expenses that come up.

I have only begun watching the show recently, but every episode I've watched I am so incredibly impressed with how they engage their clients. Both Drew, who is the realtor who finds the homes, and Jonathon, who is the contractor and does all the renovations, are always calm and cool, regardless of what comes up.

A couple may be being extremely unrealistic in what they are expecting Drew to find in a certain neighborhood, within a specific budget and with certain requirements. He calmly tells them it's unrealistic. The clients disagree, they argue with him. They tell him what they want.

He doesn't argue back. He remains calm. He then shows them houses that have everything they want in that neighborhood and are WAY over their budget. Instead of arguing with them and telling them they're wrong, he does the work-extra work at that, finds houses that will help him prove his point, and then the couple inevitably comes to the same conclusion. The Scott Brothers clearly know how to serve their clients well.

Sometimes the client may increase their budget in order to get what they want. Other times they modify their expectations and come to realize what Drew has been telling them all along is true.

Both Drew and Jonathan are always in a positive mindset, regardless of the challenges, the expectations, or whatever comes their way. They are pleasant, they use humor when talking with their clients, especially when discussing a potentially difficult subject. And they always involve the children of the couple in the process. They address all the family members by name and make them feel totally involved.

Just watching the show Property Brothers makes one want to buy a house through them. Drew and Jonathon are so skilled in reading their clients, understanding their needs and wants and exceeding them above and beyond the wildest dreams. The client is always blown away at the end result with Drew and Jonathon. They make the process less stressful, and more fun and exciting. It is such a pleasure to watch what great customer experience really is possible. If you've never watched the show, I highly recommend that you do. You will learn much about great customer engagement.

What do customers want?

Whether I'm going to a restaurant for dinner, or staying at a hotel on vacation, or going to an urgent care center for a check-up, I, as the customer have certain expectations of that experience.

I, as your customer, have expectations of how I should be treated and engaged.

I want to be treated as a human being and not merely as a transaction. I want to be acknowledged and shown respect.

I want the service I'm paying for to be delivered with some enthusiasm and care. I want the service I'm paying for to be of a certain level of quality.

I am not an account, I'm not a case, a file, or a policy number.

I am not a transaction, I'm not a subscriber.

I am your customer. I am your client. I am your patient. I am your guest.

I chose your place of business out of all the possible options available to me. I would like you to appreciate me as a person and not just thank me for my business.

I would like you to introduce yourself to me. I would like you to smile sincerely and show warmth. I am here to experience the specific service you provide.

Whether I'm getting my car's oil changed, or I'm traveling on your airline, whether I'm purchasing a thousand dollar suit, or ordering a cup of coffee, I am your customer. I am spending my (hard earned) money with you.

I am showing support and appreciation and valuing your business.

I want to feel that you acknowledge, appreciate and value me as your customer in return.

Chapter 10

ENERGY & EMOTION (PART 2)

"All of us, as humans are wired to do good."

Olivier de Roany,
Founder, CEO-Groopzoom

When my book, *Getting to WOW! Everybody WINS with 5 Star Service*, was released in January 2015, we began holding free seminars to share the content. These seminars were the launching pad for both the book and our company, ASPIRE Enterprises. At one of those first seminars, I invited my friend and at that time, Las Vegas restaurant executive, Olivier de Roany, to be our guest speaker. It was at that seminar when I heard Olivier make the above statement.

We are wired to do good. All of us are. We all know what that means. When we help someone out, when we do a favor, when we are of service to our fellow human beings-we feel good. Certainly, the recipient of our kindness feels good, but we who are serving them feel good also.

They say it's more blessed to give than receive. Well, the paradox is that when we give to others, we also always receive. That's right, doing good makes us feel good. In chapter 1 we introduced the topic of Energy and Emotion. It's all energy. It's all connected and we're all connected and it all comes back to us.

When we give to one another-and that is what we are doing when we serve, it comes back to us. Whether you're selling someone a car, or you're showing a client a house, whether you're crafting a cocktail for your bar patron, or you're teaching in a classroom, whether you're helping someone plan their retirement, or you're giving someone a massage, or speaking to a room of thousands-you are giving to them.

You are serving them. You are giving of yourself, your time, your talents, your energy-both physical and emotional. We are all connected. The positive energy that you put into your work, the positive energy that you give out, comes back to you in feelings of love and other positive emotions. We feel good about ourselves when we know we've served another person.

So, what exactly is going on here? What is causing us to feel good about serving others? Partly it is energy, but it's also something more.

Certainly, as stated before, we can consciously choose to raise our own vibration. We can elevate our energetic state. We can generate our own positive energy and positive feelings consciously. But we are also talking about something else here.

I am not a scientist, nor an expert on the subject, but I do have a basic understanding of what's happening and I'd like to share it with you. But first, let me ask you a question.

In my seminars, I typically will pose the following question to the audience, but I tell them to please do not respond until I complete the entire question. And then I begin, "How many of you have ever been high…"

As the words come out of my mouth, I see various ones looking at each other as they ponder what I'm saying. I remind them to wait until I've completed the question. I repeat and continue, "How many of you have ever been high at work…"

I pause. Now many in the audience are snickering, making silent comments. Some have even raised their hands timidly.

Again, I remind them to wait until I've completed the entire question.

I proceed, "Not artificially induced? How many of you have ever been high at work, not artificially induced?"

Now almost everyone's hand shoots up into the air.

We've all had those situations when we are in the zone. We are focused, we may have been slammed, super busy at work, but we are unaware of the time passing, the difficulty of the challenge we may have been facing, or any physical discomfort we may have had when we began. We are simply, as Tony Robbins, says, "In state". You didn't remember or realize that earlier you may have felt tired or had a pain in your back or something similar. All that is gone now. You are in the flow.

You may be a nurse taking care of a constant stream of patients in the ER for hours without a break. You may be a bartender serving drinks on New Year's Eve at the busiest bar or restaurant in Las Vegas or New York City from 3pm to 3am. Maybe you're a first responder, a teacher, an engineer, a salesman-whatever it may be, you are in the zone. You are flying high as you serve your clientele in your particular arena. Maybe you are putting on your own seminar and you are the main speaker, speaking for 5, 6, or 8 hours.

You are focused on your work, you are getting it done. You are feeling so amazing. You should have no energy left, yet here you are doing your thing. You're rocking it. You're killing it. You are high. But not on drugs. No, you've got what I call Happiness Chemicals flowing through you.

There are at least 4 chemicals which I call 'Happiness Chemicals' which are produced in our body and distributed through our bloodstream that have a powerful affect upon our emotions and also our physical bodies.

HAPPINESS CHEMICALS

1. **Endorphins-**

Endorphins are created in our central nervous system and in the pituitary gland. Endorphins are known to be a natural pain killer/ pain reliever. They are released during exercise, emotional stress and strenuous activity.

When endorphins are released into our bloodstream, we are put into a heightened emotional state. Another term for that feeling would be, we feel high. In fact, this is what is happening when one talks of the runner's high.

So, when we are in the zone at work and we are doing what we are wired to do-do good and serve others-we will have endorphins coursing through our body.

I believe this may be why some people working side by side at the same company, doing the same job, may have completely contrasting feelings and emotional states. One person is completely in the zone, they are swamped, they are being killed, but because they actually love what they do, the endorphins are kicking in and they are enjoying it. It doesn't matter how tired their body should feel, they are loving what they are doing so they just keep going, and at the end those endorphins are making them feel great.

The other person who is doing the same work, does not have a passion for it and is simply doing the job. They're not seeing it as service. It's not where they want to be nor what they wish to be doing. This person at the end of such a grueling shift and strenuous work, is not high on Happiness Chemicals. Rather they are just miserable and exhausted.

Endorphins can also be stimulated in us by eating chocolate or spicy foods.

2. Serotonin

This Happiness Chemical is derived from tryptophan-remember the protein molecule that makes people fall asleep from eating too much turkey on Thanksgiving? Serotonin is found in the gastrointestinal tract, the central nervous system and in blood platelets. It is linked to happiness and maintains mood balance. This well-being chemical comes to us through exercise and sunlight. Think of how good you feel after you've gone for a run outside on a beautiful, sunny day, or after you've don yoga in nature or just after going for a stimulating hike? That feeling of well-being you're experiencing is because Serotonin is being released into your body.

Here's another really cool and interesting fact; Serotonin is related to recognition. Knowing that, now consider the following. We live in a digital age and social media is how many people connect with others. We post pictures on Instagram, put status updates on Facebook, we constantly check our Twitter feed and look to see how many connections we have on LinkedIn.

Michelle and I have 3 puppies, Lilly, Carly and Bruno. Our children, she has 3, I have 2, are grown and so our puppies are now our babies. I often post pictures of our puppies on Facebook. I'm sure you probably have done this too, maybe of your children. If there's a picture that I'm particularly proud of, after posting it, I will check a little while later to see how many likes, shares and comments it received. I'm sure you get what I'm talking about. I get excited each time I see more people liking, sharing and commenting on my post. When they do and I see that, Serotonin is being released into my body.

Serotonin, as I mentioned, is related to giving and receiving of recognition and the corresponding feelings it generates. You may say yes, Christoff, I concur. I've experienced the same thing but what does this have to do with the Customer Experience?

First, consider how often you as a leader are giving praise and recognition to your team members. This is not merely an exercise. It actually has a powerful positive effect upon the individual receiving the recognition. We'll discuss more about recognition in a moment, but first let me finish telling you about the other two Happiness Chemicals.

3. Dopamine-

This Happiness Chemical is released by the hypothalamus and its main role is in Reward Motivated Behavior. Since Dopamine is connected to the reward center of our brain, it helps us not only to see rewards but also drives us to take action or move towards them.

When we set goals and achieve them-that feeling of accomplishment, that feeling of pride in knowing what you've done, is the result of Dopamine being released into your body.

People who are risk takers and thrill seekers are very familiar with the sensation that Dopamine gives them.

Dopamine is also connected with addictive behavior. In fact, that's where the term 'dope' for drugs came from. But addictive behavior can be both negative and positive. If you set goals with corresponding incentives for your team, there will be some people who will be attracted to and motivated by that, and they will perform better because they like the feeling that such achievement and accomplishment gives them. So, is it possible for one to be addicted to their work? Can someone actually be addicted to service, to doing good for others?

I have worked for many years in service and hospitality and I loved it. When I became an author and began training and doing public speaking I found another passion that I truly love. However, there have been many times when I have missed the feeling I get when I physically serve people in a restaurant setting. There is something dynamic and special about the interaction, the connection with the guests. I guess when I'm doing training and public speaking, I'm getting my Happiness Chemicals from the Endorphins and when I'm physically serving guests, I'm getting more of a dose of Serotonin.

There is one more Happiness Chemical that we need to discuss here, Oxytocin.

4. Oxytocin

Oxytocin is known as the 'Hug Hormone' or the 'Snuggle Drug'. It is produced in the hypothalamus and released by the pituitary gland. Oxytocin is related to feelings of love and trust.

According to an online article by Stephanie Pappas for Live Science,

"It is released when people snuggle up or bond socially. Even when playing with your dog can cause an Oxytocin surge."

This powerful hormone/Happiness Chemical is released when we truly connect, or bond with someone. When you meet someone and you feel a very deep connection with them, or when you gaze into your partner's eyes and you experience that feeling of love and trust-that is Oxytocin running through you.

Another way that Oxytocin is released is by touch, such as a hand on the shoulder or even a firm handshake. Something so simple can be so powerful.

Understanding these 4 Happiness Chemicals can go a long way to helping us elevate the customer experience. In the case of Oxytocin, am I saying that we all should hug all of our customers for them to have a feeling of well-being? Of course not. However, there certainly may be times depending on the situation, when that may be appropriate. You must of course, use wise discretion. It may not be a hug that is right in the moment, but a firm handshake and looking one in their eyes and smiling, as you extend a welcome, can have the same affect as a hug.

When we think of Serotonin and its affects upon us and our teams, we can remind ourselves of the power of appreciation and recognition. We all can do better in showing, giving appreciation a little more often to the people who are important to us.

I'm always impressed with the ways my wife, leads her team at the hospital where she works. The motto of the hospital is, "Patient and family focused care". One thing that Michelle established early on when she was promoted to leadership is an employee recognition board which is located at the entrance of the family waiting area.

This board has pictures of the nursing team in the hospital as well as them in activities outside of work. The top of the board reads, "Get to know the family that cares for your family". The board has pictures of team members who have birthdays that month, as well as a team member of the month.

I've never asked any of Michelle's team what they think about the board, but I imagine it causes them to feel good when they see it. Especially when it's their birthday or when they've been chosen as team member of the month. I also imagine that when patient's family members look at this board, they can see that the nursing team that is caring for them is filled with real people who also have families. They are not just cold medical professionals wearing scrubs. They truly care about each patient. By giving recognition and appreciation to your team, they will be more adept to do the same for your customers.

To quote my friend and mentor, Casey Eberhart, "People appreciate being appreciated."

I've said it before and I'll state it again, "The desired outcome of any interaction with your customer is always a positive feeling." It's as simple as that. So, I must ask you, how are you making your customers feel?

HOW ARE YOU MAKING YOUR GUESTS FEEL?

Ignored	Welcomed
Neglected	Appreciated
Overlooked	Acknowledged
Forgotten	Attended to
Disrespected	Honored
Disregarded	Engaged
Dismissed	Entertained
Taken for Granted	Recognized
Stressed	Relieved
Discouraged	Encouraged
Frustrated	Celebrated

With the above chart in mind, another very important point I'll always mention in my seminars, and I encourage you to write this down and remember is:

You must always be asking yourself WTF?

Hold on, it's not what you think.

WTF? You ask.

Yes, always ask yourself, WTF?

No, it's not, "What's that for?"

No, it's not, "Why's that funny?"

It's not, "Where's the folder?"

It does not mean "Wednesday, Thursday, Friday"

WTF? simply means:

"What's the Feeling?"

What's the feeling your customer is walking in with? Remember the Emotional Set Point?

Also ask yourself, WTF, What's the Feeling as they're leaving?

Hopefully the feeling they leave with is an elevated feeling to what they came in with.

Our energy, and emotions are linked. One affects the other. Our positive attitude, our positive energy, creates positive emotions within each one of us.

As we engage our customers, that energy resonates with them and affects their emotional state-their well-being.

We always have the opportunity to choose to raise our own vibration. We must consciously choose to feel great, positive, upbeat, so we can be a channel of blessing to those whom we serve.

Chapter 11

EMPATHY

Empathy is...
Seeing with the eyes of another
Listening with the ears of another
and
Feeling with the heart of another

What is empathy? Is it a skillset, a mindset, a natural intuition that certain people are gifted with? I believe it is all of the above.

One definition I read states,

> *Empathy is the action of understanding, being aware of, being sensitive to, and vicariously experiencing the feelings, thoughts, and experience of another, of either the past or the present without having the feelings, thoughts, and experience fully communicated in an objectively explicit manner.*

Considering the above definition, it is clear that empathy is both a feeling and an action. It is the choice to feel, to understand what another person is feeling, thinking or experiencing. We all have empathy. We all have the capacity to empathize. However, empathy, I believe, is a mental and an emotional muscle, if we do not exercise it often it will not come to us naturally. It really takes a conscious effort. The more we exercise our empathy muscle, the easier it will be for us to show empathy to others. If you've never been an empathetic person, it's not easy to conjure it up. It will and does take practice, but you certainly can and are able to.

One of my favorite books is entitled *Aspire*, by Kevin Hall. It is a profound book that talks about the power of words. One of the words he uncovers for us is 'Empathy'. He shares the etymology of it, saying that,

"it springs from the soil, 'pathy' comes from *path,* and 'em' is *in*. Empathy is *walking on the path of another.* If you don't get on another's path, if you don't go where he or she has gone, you can't truly understand what that person is experiencing."

Having empathy is such a critical part of the customer experience, for without it, we may be guilty of just going through the motions. Having or showing empathy is communicating to that other individual that you are there for them, you care for them and you are aware of what they're feeling or going through. You may be thinking that showing empathy does not apply in every business interaction. Perhaps you think that showing empathy is only reserved for nurses, and counselors and clergy and therapists. I disagree. Regardless of what industry you are in, showing empathy to your customers is a powerful way to connect with them.

Empathy is not always verbal. You can communicate much with a simple smile and a handshake. You don't necessarily have to say the words, "I'm here for you" to the other person. It's really about being in tune with that other person. Sending out energy that resonates with them. The other person need not necessarily be in pain, or trauma or some terrible circumstance for you show empathy. Choosing to show empathy means choosing to feel what the other person feels, their pain, their challenges, their sorrow, their joy, their triumph.

Perhaps we can't all be so completely in tune that we feel exactly what another is feeling, or experiencing. However, it begins with a choice to want to connect with them. Once we've made the conscious choice, we can then begin to feel what it's like to be in the other person's shoes.

According to Karla McLaren, author of *The Art of Empathy:*

"Empathy is a social and emotional skill that helps us feel and understand the emotions, circumstances, intentions, thoughts and needs of others, such that we can offer sensitive, perceptive and appropriate communication and support."

When I do trainings at the Bartenders Union in Las Vegas, I always ask the class, this very simple question,

"Why do people come to your bar or restaurant?"

The first reply I inevitably hear from some of them is,

"To get drunk".

While it may be true that some patrons get drunk at a bar, that is rarely the reason they go to a bar. Each guest that sits at a bar whether alone, or with other people, is there for some other underlying reason aside from 'to get drunk'.

For some they're feeling sad and they want to drown their sorrows, forget about their problems. The getting drunk part is just the medium they are using to accomplish the goal of changing the way they are feeling, temporarily.

Another patron may be lonely and they're hoping to strike up a conversation with the bartender or they're seeking companionship. Someone else may be in a celebratory mood and he's waiting for his group of friends to celebrate his new promotion. A different group of people may have gathered at your location to remember a loved one who's death anniversary is on this day. Or maybe they just came because they want to relax at the end of a long work day or week.

There's a myriad of underlying reasons which are usually linked to a specific emotion or set of emotions that person or group of people are feeling or a certain feeling they are seeking to feel. Sometimes the reason is apparent, obvious and stated aloud. "It's my birthday!" "I just got promoted!" "My girlfriend just broke up with me". Other times the reason is subtle, hidden and not clear.

As Service Professionals, we must learn to be more empathetic or in tune with our customers. The better we become at connecting with them on a deeper level, the better we'll be able to serve their needs and not only meet, but far exceed their expectations.

One of the people I interviewed for *The Customer Experience* was Lynn Belcher, former CNO -Chief Nursing Officer at a major hospital in Las Vegas. She told me about how important it is for nurses and medical staff to not see patients merely as the patient lying in that bed, stripped of their dignity, their clothes, their possessions. She said, "We have to realize that before they came in here to the hospital, they had an entire life, position at a company, a family, friends, status, reputation and more. If you can figure that out, and relate to them on that level, you'll be more therapeutic to them." (my paraphrase)

Lynn told me the story of a patient that had been having an extended stay at the hospital and to drive her point home to encourage her nursing team to be more empathetic, not just to him, but to all their patients she did something a little out of the ordinary. She had a life-size cut out made of this particular patient, made from a photo of him before he was admitted. She asked her team, "Who is this man?" She didn't want them to say, "He's Smith in 322". She wanted them to find out, to learn, to understand who is this man?

This man was a world-renowned concert violinist, who played all the biggest concert halls in the world. He was someone who was used to having the spotlight on him. He was accustomed to receiving standing ovations from thousands of adoring fans all over the world. He had a family. He had a career. He had a purpose in life. Now he was Smith in 322.

The purpose of the life-size cut out was for the nursing team to put a real face to this man that was now their patient. To know who he is outside of this hospital. To show empathy.

I agree with Lynn Belcher, if we can figure out who our customers, patients, clients, guests, are outside of here-the place where we've met them in our business, we can connect with them in a more meaningful way. That to me is what empathy is all about.

> *"Empathy has no script. There is no right way or wrong way to do it. It's simply listening, holding space, withholding judgement, emotionally connecting that incredibly healing message of 'You're not alone.'"*
>
> Anonymous

Showing empathy may come more naturally to some than to others. That is a given. It seems to me that a lot of people who are in nursing or other healing fields tend to be naturally empathetic. For others, like myself, I would say that I have empathy but it has to be more of a conscious decision. I often have to remind myself to be more empathetic. I know how important it is so, I make an effort to work on it. I know that I have a long way to go but at least I'm aware of it. That's really the first step, is to be conscious that we must meet our customers where they are at, on their level.

Let us strive to serve our customers by connecting with them beyond the surface level. Having empathy is about walking in the other person's shoes. It's about seeing the situation from another person's perspective, and being open to feel the emotions they are feeling.

To quote Lynn Belcher again, she explained to me how sometimes if she observed a nurse seemingly not showing compassion to a patient she would encourage them to "Spend one day in the life of a patient. You can't eat when you want or do what you want. You have to call and ask for permission and assistance to eat and even to use the bathroom. Everything you do is being observed and recorded."

When we put ourselves in the place of our customer or client, it will begin to spark empathy within us. The more we are conscious of and practice being empathetic, the more our empathy muscle develops.

No matter what business we are in, if we are serving customers, we must realize that each one is so much more than a customer. They are our brothers and sisters in this grand place we call earth. Each one has a life with joys and pains, heartaches and struggles and victories. When they come into our path, as my wife, Michelle says "We become a part of their story and they become a part of ours."

We have the awesome opportunity and responsibility to care for them, to bless them and to honor them in our service to them. This is empathy.

Chapter 12

EXCELLENCE

"It has been said that Perfection is unattainable, but my experience has proven that Excellence is within our reach, and I'll choose and strive for Excellence every time"

Christoff J. Weihman,
The Customer Experience

People often make mistakes, miss the mark and mess up. We forget to call a customer who is waiting for an answer. We hit the wrong button disconnecting a customer who's been on hold for fifteen minutes. We put the wrong address on a package to be shipped, we ring in the wrong item on a customer's order and we charge them double, and God forbid, but sometimes we mistakenly give the wrong medicine to a patient. We are human. We are fallible. We make mistakes and we are imperfect beings. But our goal, our standard, what we aspire to must always be a standard of Excellence.

A person of Excellence is always a person of Excellence. The customer experience will inevitably, at some point, have missteps and imperfections. No customer expects perfection. If they do, they're not living in the real world. What I hope for is that you desire and choose to become a person of Excellence. If you take pride in how you show up to work, your attire, your attitude, your energy, your demeanor, that is going to translate into an exceptional customer experience.

I've experienced many times at a restaurant when something was not correct. I call these instances a 'Soupfly'-something that could go wrong, like a fly in your soup. I did not order soup with a fly in it. You, my server, did not put it in there, I'm hoping. And yet, there it is. But it's not the end of the world, nor is it the end of the opportunity for me to have a great dining experience. You are a person of Excellence, so what do you do? First obviously, you apologize. No finger pointing, no excuses. Just take responsibility and own it. "I am so sorry, sir. We are not known for serving flies in our soup. Please accept my apology."

Then what? Make sure you tell the manager and let's move on. Bring me something that you know I will enjoy. If I'm vegan-I am, then do not offer to bring me your finest ribeye. If I'm gluten-free, my wife is, don't offer to bring me your best fettucine alfredo. A person of Excellence is always a person of Excellence.

If you don't take pride in how you answer the phone or set the table, how can I be sure that you are diligent in communicating my dietary needs and allergies to the chef when you place my order?

One of my favorite mentors, T. Harv Eker, author of *Secrets of the Millionaire Mind*, says,

"How you do anything, is how you do everything."

And as my wife is fond of saying and reminding me, "A person of Excellence is always a person of Excellence."

I think she is quoting me when she says that. No matter.

Your pursuit of excellence should carry through to every aspect of your work. This includes how you communicate with your customers. Excellence should be your standard in all you do, not just when someone is looking. Excellence and integrity are inextricably linked. You can't have one without the other.

If, we don't make a conscious decision to be excellent and to do excellent-that is, do things in an excellent manner, then we are cheats. We are cheating others of the quality work we should be doing. We are cheating others of our great talents, wonderful personalities, great senses of humor, extensive knowledge, amazing insights and kindheartedness. Whatever your gift or calling is-it is your responsibility to do that to the best of your ability. Why? Because your gift is not for you. What? I'll say it again. Your Gift Is Not For You. Yes, that's exactly true.

You may be saying, "What do you mean? That does not make sense. If they're not mine, then whose are they?"

Answer: Your gifts are for everyone else. Your gifts, your talents, your passion, though they may be things that give you joy, happiness and satisfaction-you are supposed to be a blessing to others via those gifts. They're not just for you. So, when you are not sharing your gifts, when you are not doing your best, putting forth your all, doing things in an excellent manner you are depriving others, your customers, who are meant to be the beneficiaries of them.

Excellence is NOT Perfection

We are not expecting perfection. We are expecting excellence. Striving for excellence allows for room to grow. Like my friend James Dently often says, "The largest room in the world is the room for improvement."

We all can get better every day, as we strive for and make Excellence our standard. Excellence is not perfection, however, average is never acceptable. Don't say or think or have the mindset of "It's okay". No its not. Okay is not okay. Okay is mediocre.

Excellence is Contagious

When you commit to Excellence, that commitment will shine through and it will cause others to follow suit. You will positively affect those around you as you make Excellence your standard. You will be an inspiration to your colleagues and your peers. Your customers will be attracted to you and will come back for more because they know what you stand for and strive for.

A championship team is made up of many champions, not just one superstar. This is as true in business as it is in sports. Michael Jordan led his team, the Chicago Bulls, to six National Championships. He set a standard of Excellence for his team. Yes, he was the leader, but his team members rose to that standard of Excellence set for them.

A few final thoughts about Excellence:

Excellence is NOT a sometime thing.

Excellence is not something you do when you are periodically, or once in a while, inspired to greatness. Excellence must be a daily habit.

Excellence is Contagious. You will affect, inspire and motivate others as you set an example with your commitment to Excellence.

Excellence must show up in your communication with your customers; how you treat them, talk to them, the care and manner in which you sell to them and serve them.

Excellence means you follow up and you follow through. Don't just give it your all one time. Build an ongoing connection with your clientele with Excellence as the foundation and integrity as the mortar that holds the structure firmly together.

Achieving Excellence in anything comes from a conscious commitment and making it a daily habit. Why is Excellence so important? Two reasons;

1. Because that is who you are, your true nature is Excellence,
2. Because your customers deserve it.

Every customer deserves to receive excellent service.

I believe this so strongly that this is what I have printed on the back of my business card:

Every Customer Deserves to Receive Five Star Service

Do Your Customers Consistently Receive it?

Deliver 5 Stars=Reap 5 R's

Repeat Customers, Referrals, Reviews, Reputation, Revenue

When you live a life of Excellence, you are being your Greatest Possible Self, GPS, and like my friend Chris Burns says,

"How do you truly stand out in your customer's eyes? Choose to show up being your Greatest Possible Self (GPS). When you're being your best, focusing on excellence, and giving world-class service, people will notice, they will remember how you made them feel, and they will definitely want more."

I completely agree with my friend, Chris Burns. Do you?

Where in your business can you raise the standard higher?

Are you leading your team with an attitude and mindset that Excellence is your goal, all the time, every time?

What areas have you allowed average to creep in and you now choose to set the bar at Excellence?

Chapter 13

EXECUTION

Putting it all together

It is in the synergistic application of all components that the Customer Experience comes to life.

I find it very interesting that in today's slang when someone has done a job or a task well, we use the phrase "They killed it". I first heard this term when I was doing standup comedy in Los Angeles. If a comic really connected with the audience and did well, "They killed". If they did poorly, "They bombed".

One definition of execution is: "The carrying out of or putting into effect a plan, order or course of action"

Now we've come to that point where we must put all the pieces together. The Customer Experience is much more than the sum of a bunch of disparate parts. The Customer Experience is a Journey with sometimes a few, sometimes many, other times-countless Touchpoints. These Touchpoints are our opportunities to positively impact those on the Journey.

As we mentioned at the outset, we must master our own **Energy and Emotions** and learn to raise our vibration so that we are connecting with our customers in a positive manner. However, before we even connect with our customers, there are many steps we must take to ensure that we are Consciously Creating and Elevating the Emotional Journey for our Customers.

Let us **Envision** a clear picture of what kind of Experience we want our customers to have.

Next, we will attract and assemble a Team of like-minded and like-hearted individuals who resonate with our **Employment** ideals and our organization's vision, mission and goals.

We will then train, equip and **Empower** this amazing team to carry out that vision and mission by serving our customers according to our core values- which is our promise to them.

After they've been Empowered, we must ensure that each one is on board, by **Enlisting** their commitment, and helping them realize that each one of them plays a vital role in the overall success of the organization.

We will consciously create/control our **Environment** to ensure that it is conducive to creating the Experience that we desire for all of our customers, (both internal and external). We do this with the effective and intentional use of color, lighting, sound, aroma, temperature and the physical surroundings.

Our standard of Excellence for ourselves and our Teams will be our guide as to how we anticipate, meet and supercede/exceed our Customers' **Expectations**.

By consistently, maintaining high levels of real **Engagement** with our Team members, they in turn will be more fully **Engaged** with our Customers to Serve them well.

As we choose to show **Empathy** to our Customers, we understand that we can positively affect how they feel. Or at least we can share in the experience that they are having, if we are not able to affect it.

We do not expect Perfection of ourselves or others, but we do strive daily for **Excellence** in all we do. We also agree that Excellence is the standard that all our customers deserve.

We are constantly aware of the importance of both self-**Evaluation** and asking for input and feedback from our Customers. We openly receive this information, realizing that the customer's perception of their experience is their reality. We use this feedback to celebrate our wins, and to know what areas we can focus upon and improve.

By putting all these pieces together, by working in harmony, we Consciously Create and Elevate the Emotional Journey for all whom we serve.

We acknowledge, recognize, embrace and declare that together, and individually,

We Are the Customer Experience.

Chapter 14

EVALUATION

*"Let's face it, no one cares what you think of your business!
They want to know what everyone else thinks about your
company. Let your happy customers sell for you."*

-Trevor Howard-
SoTellUs

W e all believe that we do our job well, that we perform to the best
of our ability and certainly, self-evaluation has its place. However,
if we truly want honest, unfiltered feedback, if we really want to
know if we are hitting the mark in serving our customers we should
just ask them.

In my first book, *Getting to WOW!*, I have a subchapter entitled,
Getting Your Customers to Complain. In it I talk about how in the
restaurant business it is crucially important to make sure your guests
are voicing their complaints in a timely manner-before they leave your
building. Why is this? Because once they've left your establishment you
may be able to respond to their complaint, but the opportunity to fix
the problem is lost forever. I would say that this goes for any type of
business. If one has a complaint, we must address it as soon as possible
and preferably, while your customer is still having the experience. This
is why in the chapter on Engagement we stressed the importance of

'Touching Tables'. You may use a different term in your industry but the concept is the same. Management must make every effort to be aware of what is going on in their place of business.

I remember distinctly the two restaurants that I worked for when I lived in St. Louis. Both were fine dining restaurants. One had guest survey cards placed in every guest checkbook that was placed on the table. We were not only *encouraged* to invite our guests to fill out the survey card, we were *required* to make sure that we retrieved the check and survey card *before* the guests exited the restaurant. This was not always easy to do. But I was amazed and impressed with how much importance the owners of this restaurant placed on the feedback from those customer survey cards. They truly valued their customers' opinions and input.

If something negative was written on the card, a manager would talk with the customer before they left. Sometimes a customer will tell you face to face that everything was great and then, when given the opportunity to give feedback on paper they will reveal how they really feel.

The other restaurant that I worked at did not have any survey cards at all. I remember one time talking with the owner about survey cards and suggested that they might be a good way to get customer feedback. His response was, "All those things do is create problems-it gives the customer an invitation to complain." It was no surprise that the first restaurant consistently had 4 ½ stars on Yelp while the other hovered between 3 and 3 ½ stars.

Contrary to what the owner of the 2nd restaurant believed, those survey cards at the first restaurant, more often than not, were filled with praises for the experience that the customers had, they loved the food and they loved the service. Did having those survey cards on every table cause our staff to be more conscientious in how we served our guests? I believe so. Certainly, it had a subconscious impact on us. But it also communicated to our guests that we care, that we have certain standards, and that those standards were our promise to our guests.

The Importance and Power of Reviews

There are many forums and ways to solicit and receive reviews from your customers. Many industries have a review site that is specific to them. For example, for attorneys there's AVO, or Martindale, for wedding industry professionals there's The Knot and Wedding Wire, for hotels and travel sites there's Trip Advisor and for restaurants there's Yelp. Actually, any business can receive a review on Yelp or Google.

Are there fake reviews on these sites? Of course, there may be. And do we take as gospel truth every point made by a customer reviewing their experience at a place of business? NO. However, we must accept that their perception is their experience. So, is it important for us to take review sites seriously? Absolutely. In fact, I would go one step further and say that we should embrace the reviews.

Remember the question we must always be asking ourselves? WTF? What's the feeling? If we keep that forefront in our minds, then we and our entire team will take more care when serving our customers.

Customer feedback is valuable because it helps us know what we are doing very well and on what areas we can improve. It also reveals opportunities for growth that you may want to invest in specific training for your team.

Reviews can be very powerful tools. In fact, they can be one of the best marketing tools available to you. Your loyal followers, your committed customers, those who love how you serve them, they are your best evangelists. They are your unpaid, highly motivated marketers. They will willingly, freely sing your praises if you invite them to and you make it easy for them.

SOTELLUS

One of my favorite review sites is called SoTellus. You like our service? SoTellus about it. You had an amazing time at our resort? SoTellus about it. Christoff J. Weihman gave an amazing, inspiring keynote at your conference? SoTellus about it. SoTellus is the only video customer review system out there. They are revolutionary. Their platform is so simple to use and so powerfully effective.

Established by father and sons team, Ron Howard and his two sons, Trevor and Troy, SoTellus, is changing how customers do reviews. It is a simple app that allows one to record on their own phone, a video review of a business, service or person. The video then can be set to automatically populate on your company's own website and all your social media platforms.

It is a brilliant tool. I use it for my books, and for my speaking and training. A positive video review by your customers will speak volumes more about you and the quality of your work and service you provide than you could ever convey on your website. Why? Because it's your customers talking and raving about you, not you talking about how great you are. A SoTellus review is your real life customers expressing their appreciation for your product or service.

If you own a business, I highly recommend you consider using SoTellus to capture in real time video reviews from your customers. If you are providing an excellent service to your customers, then others need to know about it. There is nothing more powerful than a video review from a happy customer who just had an amazing experience with your business.

*See ad in back of book to start capturing SoTellus reviews for your business.

Chapter 15

ENRICHMENT (OF OTHERS) & ENLIGHTENMENT (OF ONE'S SELF)

"Our highest calling is to use our gifts in Service to others. The world is waiting for you to heed the call."

Christoff J. Weihman

The Spiritual Aspect of Service

I f you are called to serve, and I believe we all are- we must each accept and embrace that calling. Whatever industry you may be in, whatever role you're invited to play, you have a gift. And that gift is not meant to be kept hidden. Don't hide your light under a bushel basket.

Your gift was given to you for you to be a blessing to, and to enrich others. In whatever manner you serve, aspire to be your greatest possible self. In so doing, we are practicing ministry. We are performing a spiritual practice when we embrace our call to serve.

Whatever profession you are in, whether you're an employee or an entrepreneur, if you are engaging with customers, you are in service.

Whether you're a plumber, or an attorney, a social media marketer or a nurse, whether you're a motivational speaker or a missionary, a chef or a photographer, whether you're an auto mechanic or a writer, a postal worker or a pastor, you are in service. And service is ministry.

What you do is so much more than the specific task or duty you perform. You have a gift to share and that gift is you being your greatest possible self. You are a special and unique human being and only you have the calling, the ability, the power and the responsibility to share that gift-your particular gift, with the world.

The Service you provide is greater than the task being performed. You are doing so much more than even creating an exceptional experience for your customers.

You are ministering to their spirits, uplifting them, bringing them joy and happiness and creating positive feelings for them. You are being a channel of blessing. Every day you have the opportunity to create powerful, positive, lasting memories *for* them and *with* them.

And it all comes back to you-the positive emotions, and positive energy, the happiness chemicals and financially, knowing that you made a difference in someone's day, or life, being the deliverer of a consciously created and elevated experience for them unlike no other, because you realize that…

YOU ARE THE CUSTOMER EXPERIENCE.

Service is about giving. Ever since *Getting to WOW!* was first published, we have taken a portion of the profits of the book sales and given to non-profits and charities that do amazing, self-less work, serving those in need. Whether it be Three Square Foodbank in Las Vegas, or House of Neighborly Service in Loveland, Colorado or other non-profits, we have always shared with others from our book sales. With *The Customer Experience*, we will be doing likewise. A portion of all profits will be donated to Non-profits that I support and whose mission resonates with me. Your purchase of this book contributes to supporting these amazing organizations. I am grateful for your support.

For more information on these organizations go to:

Christoffjweihman.com

Author's Resources

The following are books by authors that have positively influenced me. I have referred to them or quoted them in *The Customer Experience*, or I just highly recommend them to you:

Amaze Every Customer Every Time-Shep Hyken
Aspire-Kevin Hall
Ask and It is Given-Esther & Jerry Hicks
Be Obsessed or Be Average-Grant Cardone
Be Your Customer's Hero-Adam Toporek
Getting to WOW! -Christoff J. Weihman
Sacred Commerce-Matthew & Terces Engelhart
Secrets of the Millionaire Mind-T. Harv Eker
The Advantage-Patrick Lencioni
The Art of Empathy-Karla McLaren
The Charge-Brendon Burchard
The 4 Disciplines of Execution-Chris McChesney, Sean Covey, Jim Huling
Three Signs of a Miserable Job-Patrick Lencioni
Think and Grow Rich-Napoleon Hill
7 Easy Steps to Write Your Book-Ann McIndoo